BEVERLY GI

Slow Down
and _Simplify_

Easy steps to
rediscovering
peace
in your life

Pacific Press® Publishing Association
Nampa, Idaho
Oshawa, Ontario, Canada

Edited by Kenneth R. Wade
Cover and inside design by Michelle C. Petz

Copyright ©1998 by
Pacific Press® Publishing Association
Printed in the United States of America
All Rights Reserved

Stickle, Beverly Graham, 1944-
    Slow down and simplify : buy people share tips for rediscovering peace
in your life / Beverly Graham Stickle.
        p.   cm.
    ISBN 0-8163-1688-0
    1. Simplicity.   2. Stress management.   I. Title.
BJ1496.S75   1998
646.7—dc21   98-34112
                                                                        CIP

98 99 00 01 02 • 5 4 3 2 1

Dedication

For my mother, Margaret Graham, whose life I have never simplified but who loves and supports me anyway.

Contents

Acknowledgments

Marian Forschler, thank you for your encouragement, suggestions, and editing. Thank you for being such an inspiration to everyone. Your sense of humor and advice are invaluable.

Thanks to Art Klym, my brother-in-law, for your advice on wills.

J. T. and Bonnie Shim, my Florida friends. Thank you for your ideas and suggestions. Although we have never met, you were kind enough to spend hours doing the original editing. J. T., thank you for sharing your time to help me. Bonnie, thank you for giving your input, too, and for letting J. T. spend all those hours on his computer.

Thank you, Jack and Jean Sequeira, for sharing your story.

My editor Ken Wade. Thank you for all your input, encouragement, and help. I know that editing this book didn't simplify your life!

Bonnie Starlin, thanks for your suggestions and careful editing and proofreading.

Thank you Brit Stickle for your help and support.

The more than two hundred people I interviewed, thank you for sharing your stories. Thank you for all your suggestions on how to simplify life. You gave many good ideas.

Thanks to my son, Ryan, for encouraging me to get a new computer and helping me to pick one out. That computer simplifies my life—well most of the time!

Most of all for my husband, Don. Thank you for your love, encouragement, and support. Because of all your help, I could write this book. I couldn't have done it without you!

Chapter 1

Do You Want to Simplify?

Jack and Jean were leaving from a country that was going through turmoil. They were told to pack everything. They were to make three stacks. One for keeping. One for selling (with every price marked). And the third for giving away.

Jean was up until the wee hours of the morning sorting through "stuff." It was discouraging to see how much there was that really wasn't all that important. She finally gave up and left a note on the door saying, "She hath done what she could . . ."

Imagine her surprise when she got up later and saw the following words written in a familiar hand, "Go, and sin no more!"

Acquiring more "stuff" is not necessarily a sin, Jack. But not acquiring any more might help us to simplify our lives.

"What are you doing?" my neighbor Ann asked. "I have watched you for a week. Every day you carry out garbage bags from the house."

"I'm getting rid of anything that doesn't run faster than me or isn't tied or nailed down. I'm trying to simplify my life," I answered.

Ann laughed, "Just what I need to do. But it would be so overwhelming; I don't want to start." Many people want to simplify their lives. Some buy books on how to simplify. But it makes them tired just to think about how much work it would be to read the book and take the time to change. I hope you won't feel that way about this book. I've tried to make it easy to read—a book that suggests simple ways to simplify. As you read, I hope you'll feel that you can at least try to simplify without spending too much energy, money, or time.

I think Jesus was thinking of people who need to slow down or simplify their lives when He mentioned people being "choked with cares and riches and pleasures of this life" (Luke 8:14 KJV). He knew most of us could benefit from making our lives less complicated.

I have had to simplify my life because I have to cope with four autoimmune diseases. I've discovered that everything makes a difference in my life. Just doing or not doing one little thing can make a big difference in what I can accomplish in a day. But I don't claim to be an expert with all the answers. So, in preparation for writing this book I asked others for suggestions about how to simplify life. More than two hundred people answered my questions. I've included their suggestions in the chapters that follow. I hope you find our ideas helpful. And if you have ideas you'd like to share, I'd love to hear from you. You can write me via E-mail at bevstickle@compuserve.com or BevGrahamStickle@Juno.com. Or if you prefer to write a letter, send it to me in care of:

Pacific Press Publishing Association
P. O. Box 5353
Nampa, ID 83653-5353

Chapter 2

"Simplitude"

"I'd like to cancel the next four weeks. I'm so stressed out! If I can't have an island or cabin to myself, I'd settle for being snowed in for a month!" Jamie groaned. She is married, the mother of four children, and works full time as a manager in a fast-food restaurant.

Jamie continued, "I feel like I'm going round and round like a beacon. My house is a mess. I can't always find my bills. If I take time to do my housework, I don't have time for my family. If I take time for my husband and children, I don't have time for my housework, to make meals, do laundry, or attend all the meetings I should. The list is endless. I've attended seminars on getting organized, and if I did all they said to do, all the time, there would be no time for family and friends. I need to simplify my life. In fact, I've bought three books on simplifying life, but I haven't had time to read them!"

Simplify life, Jamie? Those two words are not compatible. Life is not simple! However, there are a number of things we can do to make our lives easier. Why not make simplifying more than just cutting back things—make it an attitude. Maybe Mary had the right idea when she said, "Call it a simplitude."

How many of us are like Jamie? Do we have some areas in our lives we wish would run a little smoother? There will always be some days when we are so overwhelmed that we don't know where to start. How can we make those days fewer?

Making life easier means different things to different people. What would simplify life for some would complicate life for others.

Doug and Jane tried to simplify their lives by moving from a city to the country and doing without many modern conveniences. They love it, for the most part. But living without modern conveniences wouldn't simplify my life!

According to my dictionary, "simplify" means to show an easier or shorter process for doing something. My sister says that to her, simplifying is doing anything that would help calm her soul. So, maybe to simplify our lives might mean to do something that will help us live at peace with ourselves and have happy, fulfilled lives.

Instead of cutting back, adding something might help us achieve an inner contentment. Maybe in place of *simplify* we could say "make less complicated," "make more peaceful," "make less stressful," "make more comfortable," "make easier," or "make more fulfilling."

Subtracting and adding

True simplifying and rediscovering peace is a combination of cutting back, cutting clutter, cutting anything that is not meaningful to us, and then maybe adding something to bring delight to our souls. This doesn't mean adding so much that you become stressed out again but adding something for your inner self. Just the cutting back will bring pleasure, if that is what you need to do to simplify your life. However, many of us may need to add something to nourish our inner being—our very souls.

I think Kate expressed it best when she wrote, "I'd like to cut down on the stress and tension, to feel under less pressure, to be able to relax more."

Judy, who is retired, said the same thing, "People today are so harassed and stressed they need something to make their lives easier. I'm not talking about adding more conveniences but something to help them know they don't have to be the perfect anything or to have the perfect anything."

My friend Roberta requests, "Have a chapter on planning your funeral. It can save money and problems later." Another friend disagrees; he wrote, "In fact, my life is too complex now, why would I want to be planning something that I hope is far off—it seems like just one more task to add to my already busy life." Could planning your own funeral give you a sense of peace? Read chapter 26 and see!

Prioritize

Jeannette wrote, "I would like to have more time for family and friends and to be more spontaneous, like when I was a teen."

Lorelle, a single parent of three active children, says, "It seems when you have kids and work, you have to simplify or go nuts. My best way is to set priorities about what is actually important to get accomplished in a day. Children have a way of growing quickly. One has to maybe leave some of the cleaning a little longer and spend time with them. After they are asleep, the stuff that needs cleaning is always there. My best way of simplifying is getting my head straight about what is really important."

Yes, Lorelle. I believe you have a point. Your attitude about what is important in your life will help you decide on what needs simplifying.

What are your priorities? What is important to you?

"When trying to decide what your top priorities are," Mabel said, "nothing does it better or quicker than being told you have a fatal disease. Several years ago I was told I had a fatal disease. The doctors said I probably only had a few months to live. For one week I was deciding what really mattered to me. The next week the doctors said they had made a wrong diagnosis. I learned from that experience. Pretending you have a fatal disease can help you determine what your priorities are."

Colleen Reese, a friend and mentor who is the author of 116 books and 1,300 story articles, says, "I had to learn to simplify so I could sell over 100 books in 20 years. Simplifying is both happy and sad. Life is a tradeoff. I realized I could do the work but had to set realistic goals. In order to simplify, I had to cut down my social life, for example talking with friends, cutting down on telephone conversations, cutting down on the number of invitations I accepted, even when I wanted to go."

Mary said she'd like to simplify her life so she could have more time with her husband, children, and grandchildren.

"I want more time to do 'fun' things," Nancy wrote. "I'd really like time to make braided rugs, make quilts, work with my doll collection, and write my life story."

Ann wanted more time to do crafts.

Rose, a busy wife, mother, and director of a hospital intensive care unit, says, "I'd like to simplify my life just so I could 'get it all done.' "

"I'd like to simplify my life so I could just be plain lazy," Mindy said.

Penny agreed, "I would like more time to enjoy the pleasures of life."

A number of women wrote that they wanted more time getting to know God by studying His Word.

Maggie said she'd like to simplify her life so she could "stop working, travel more, and maybe find a millionaire to marry!"

Linette wants more time for relaxing and reading.

Some women said that because of their health, they needed to simplify their lives. Margo said, "I need to simplify so I can be less complex and cluttered. I have too much stress with having two chronic diseases."

"I have too many things to do, and it seems to keep me from

doing things with and for other people in my life," wrote Phyllis.

It is different in Sadie's life. She told me "I don't have a husband, and my children are grown and I don't have my dog anymore, so I feel my life is fairly simple." If Sadie is happy with her life, then she shouldn't have to do any simplifying. However, if she feels her life is empty, she might be one of the ones who could benefit by adding something that would make her life happier. What about having a tea party (see chapter 15) once a year or once a month for others to come and relax? It might give her something to look forward to and add pleasure to her life.

My husband agrees that it's best not to make life too simple. He says that his life is simpler when his wife has a challenge to work on. He says "I'm happier then;" and his wife says "it makes his life simpler, because, when I'm busy working on a challenge, I'm not thinking up things for him to do or noticing his shortcomings!"

Angie said, "Sometimes trying to make life more simple makes it more complicated."

Mickie agrees with Angie, "When I try to cut back, everything goes wrong."

Yes, that's true. It's possible to make the process of simplifying so complicated we either don't want to start or get bogged down in the process. It's better to start small (see chapter 3, "Simplifying Simplifying").

Quite often, like Mickie says, an incident will happen that will make us wish we hadn't started to simplify. When it does, how do we handle it?

If we can handle it like Hilda did, then we will continue to be able to simplify and improve our lives. If we get discouraged, we may end up giving up altogether.

Here's what Hilda told me.

"My friend called me, crying and upset. After about half an hour of listening to her weeping, I said, 'Rachel what you need to do is get out of the house. As soon as I shower and dress, I'll be down to get you.'

"When I went to go out the door, I looked for my car keys. Then I remembered. We had sold the car six months ago to simplify our lives and kept only my husband's truck. I called Rachel.

" 'Rachel,' I laughed. 'I can't come get you. I don't have a car! Can you imagine not having a car for six months and then I forgot!'

"Rachel laughed, 'I remembered you didn't have a car, but thought you must have kept the truck today!' "

Both Rachel and Hilda had a good laugh over this complication of simplifying. "And we both felt better," Hilda reported.

Let's keep simplifying simple, and not lose our sense of humor.

Chapter 3

Simplifying Simplifying

"The reason many of us never get beyond thinking about simplifying our lives is that we think it will be a big production to do so or have tried and it was a big production!" John said.

Mindy agrees, "I get a headache just thinking about trying to simplify my life. I think the answer for me is to take a pill and go to bed."

"If it takes all my energy to simplify my life, am I simplifying it?" Roxanne asks.

Hilda wrote, "Why simplify what you can't change?"

Maybe what we need are some ideas on how to make simplifying easier.

Simplifying your life might be as simple as skipping a TV program. Or it might be as complicated as moving to a new place or taking a new job.

When thinking about simplifying something in your life, remember to consider your health, finances, personality, and time frame. Don't try to simplify by following someone else's plan. Remember that you are an individual. Your health or finances might be different. Adapt ideas to fit your situation.

When looking at the following hints, remember that you need to pick what will work for you in your situation.

Hints for simplifying simplifying
- Think about what you want to simplify.
- Write down what you want to simplify.
- Write down how you think you can do it.
- Start with a small project or start with what's bothering you the most.
- Break the project into smaller parts.
- Reward yourself.

Think about what you want to simplify
You can do this riding in the car or waiting in a line at the grocery store. Ask yourself what do I want to simplify in my life? One example might be, housework is killing me. I'd like to start with that.

Or, you might decide to simplify a job while doing it or while trying to ignore it. For example, while cleaning the house, or ignoring the mess, you might decide housekeeping is an area you want to simplify.

Events may force you to simplify. That happened to us recently when my husband was told that his company was "downsizing." The branch in our city will be closed. He has to deal with being out of a job in another week.

Write down what you want to simplify
As you think of areas in your life that you would like to change, write them down. You might want to write them on slips of paper and put them in a jar, basket, box, or file folder. You might want to put them in a journal or notebook. This will help you remember,

and prioritize, what you want to change. You won't have to keep thinking, "Now what was it that I was going to do differently?"

Usually writing down something frees us to go on to the next step. We don't have to keep going back and making ourselves sick about what we have to simplify. We have simplified worrying about what we need to simplify!

If just the idea of writing down what you would like to simplify gives you a migraine, try making it fun. Take a break, make your favorite drink, put your feet up, and jot down some things you would like to modify. You could even do this while sitting with the family as they are watching TV.

Write down how you think you can simplify

Sometimes writing down how you are going to simplify something will make it easier for you to actually simplify it. You may have your own ideas or get ideas from hearing, reading, or seeing ways that you think might work for you. Write them down.

However, if your project is something simple like throwing away the newspaper, don't bother writing it down. Just throw away the newspaper! Don't use the writing down hint as a way to procrastinate. (You know the ploy of anything-I-can-do-to-stop-me-doing-what-I-could-be-doing-at-this-moment trick. I won't admit to how I know about that one!)

Sometimes when trying to simplify, you may think that the simplifying process is complicating your life. For example, to help yourself work on a project, you may want to get information from the library—books, cassettes, CDs, videos, or magazines. If it is going to be a complicated project, maybe the best way to make it simpler would be to attend a lecture or a class before you start. Sometimes friends have been successful at doing what you want to do—ask them.

Whatever method you choose to help you simplify, keep it simple! Do it the fastest, cheapest way.

Start with a small project or with what is bothering you the most

After you have simplified one little thing in your life, you will have the confidence to tackle something bigger.

If what is bothering you the most seems like too big a project, write it down anyway. As things come along and you think they may help, jot them down. You will at least feel like you are doing something. You might need to move on to the next tip and break the project up and work on it piece by piece. For example, take what you can work on for fifteen minutes and do that portion of the job. Thinking about and actually working for fifteen minutes is a lot easier than working for an hour or two.

Reward yourself

Most of the time reward yourself with time and fun activities instead of more things to complicate your life. For example—no candy bars! With big projects, you might want to reward yourself at fifteen-minute intervals—take a break and read a book or do something else you long for the time to do. Put the timer on. If you can't take a break exactly when it goes off, you can tally up each fifteen-minute segment and take a longer break later. Use your reward time to do something fun. This allows you to keep saying to yourself, "This might be painful now, but I can have extra time to do . . . "

A single mom might need to trade with another mom to have time to work on a project or time to reward herself. It might be fun to work on a project with a friend. Another way would be to have each person work on her own project but encourage each other then do something they might want to do together as a reward.

Reward yourself by doing something for your soul. It could be as simple as taking a tea break while in the middle of a project. It might be more complicated like decorating your bedroom or one corner of your bedroom after you have cleared it of clutter. When you choose something to do for your soul, make sure it gives you a sense of peace or serenity.

Whatever you choose to simplify, try to make it as simple and painless as possible. If you make it complicated, you might as well forget it. Mazel said, "I become overwhelmed with something then tend to run away from it."

My friend Patsy wrote, "Time for meditation and quiet thinking—putting thoughts in writing helps ease my mind and helps me put things into a simpler perspective. Often leading a simpler life means having fewer things and adopting attitudes of being content. Being agreeable with yourself and with others makes things easier. People who require all sorts of special attention and have a lot of needs and wants complicate relationships."

Terry, an office manager, gave these hints: Take an idea and try it. If it works, keep it up until it becomes a habit. Don't get discouraged.

When simplifying, try to use what you have. In most cases, it is not simplifying to add more stuff to simplify.

Make sure you are simplifying because of your priorities. You don't have to compare yourself to others.

Happy simplifying!

Chapter 4

No! No! No!

"Learn to say No and throw everything away," Carrie advised. "That will simplify your life!"

Linda advocated, "Learning to say No is OK. Just don't wait until you are forty years old to learn."

"If I learn to say No and cut back on jobs, I need also to learn to accept the consequences. I need to learn not to feel guilty if the jobs don't get done," Jenny said.

Maybe instead of singing, "Row, row, row your boat," you'll have to learn to sing "No, No, No I won't!"

"People get upset when you say No," Priscilla commented.

Melba says it is the way we say No. She says we might have to say it a different way; maybe if we said No in a kind yet assertive way, we wouldn't be afraid that we'd hurt people's feelings. Maryellen agrees. Her philosophy is to say No in a nice way. Say No and make it stick. Say No and don't feel guilty.

Many people gave me ideas on how to say No and make it stick:

- Say "I can't do that." Or "I am sorry, I'd like to do that, but I'm just not up to it at this time."
- Say "I am sorry, but I have too many other commitments right now." Or "Thanks for asking, but my time is already committed."
- Just do it. Just say No.

Two suggestions were given that might work for you but could just delay the need to finally say No.

- Say "I need to pray about it." Or
- Say "I need to talk it over with my husband" (or whomever you want to make the scapegoat).

One person says that it is not saying No he has a problem with. It's when people won't take No for an answer. Another person says that when someone won't take No for an answer, he asks them what job they will trade—what job of his they'll take.

What if like Dan you think you have learned to say No but actually have only traded jobs? Dan said he thought he had learned to say No. However, he said No to one job and then was promptly recruited to do another. It happened to Kevin too. When he got out of one job, Kevin said he took on a bigger one. Whoops! How can we stop doing that? How can we learn to say No to one job and then not take another? That was the question a number of people asked.

If you have trouble saying No, here are some tips from people who say they could and do say No. They said you will be able to say No easier if you:

- View saying No as a matter of self-preservation.
- Say No in a short conversation.
- Pick and choose what you need or want to do.
- Allow yourself to be assertive.
- Learn to limit yourself. Teach your children limits. (One woman

said she was reading and teaching a class on boundaries because she was a born caregiver.)

- Realize you can only do so much. You probably can't do a quality job if you try to do too many. You will get burned out if you do too much.
- Try to evaluate the impact on your busy life as you make your decisions.
- You are forced to say No because of your circumstances. Ann's situation is an example. This year Ann took on the job of school principal. It has more stress and responsibility than her previous job. She learned to say No and stick to it.
- Think of your priorities. Have priorities for your health, your family, and your finances.

Barbara told how she and her husband had thought of their priorities. She wrote, "We have said No to some invitations. We want to make people a priority. We have refused several social events that would be nice but would crowd our schedule. We try to say Yes and make an effort to attend specific celebrations like weddings, baby or wedding showers, funerals, birthdays."

However, what about the unexpected things that come up? "It is hard to say No to the unexpected things," June said. She gave an example. "A member of our church died. I had to be in charge of the dinner after the funeral. I also had to see that someone took care of the family. It literally took four days of my life! Sometimes we might not be able to say No. Maybe that's when we have to learn to delegate. If we divide the work into small portions, maybe more people would be willing to help."

Sometimes we might have to say No when we really want to do something and others might not understand why we are saying No. Many times I have had to say No to things that I wanted to do; for example, help someone on a project, be on a committee, or take a job in the church. From experience I know that if I don't say

No, I will get overtired. Then I have to rest and cannot do anything for the next couple of weeks or months while I get my strength back.

You may find however, that you need to say Yes to a few things, such as taking the time in the middle of a hectic week to have lunch with a friend. The warmth of the friendship could help carry you through the rest of the week.

Some people felt that the key was to learn when to say No and when to say Yes. Learning to say No doesn't mean that we will never have to do something we don't want to do or that it will give us stress. It just means that we are trying to limit the stress in our life. When we can say No it means we are in charge or trying to take charge of our lives.

Chapter 5

Taper Your Paper

"Help! I'm drowning in a paper flood!" wrote Mavis.

Yes, Mavis, if paper was snow, most of us would be ten feet under with no thaw in sight.

We can identify with Janette, who said, "If I could control the paper in my life, I would have control of my life."

"What are you doing?" my husband asked, as he watched me throw some mail into the garbage before bringing it into the house.

"I'm throwing out all the junk mail and all the catalogues for all the stores so I won't waste my time even looking at them," I replied. He didn't say anything, but I could tell he questioned my sanity. The next week he saw a neighbor lady doing the same thing.

In a surprised voice he said, "She's doing the same thing you do!"

"Yes," I answered, "quite a few people do that."

When I asked people for their tips on controlling the paper in their lives, throwing away junk mail and catalogues before they were brought into the house was the most widely used tip people gave. (Thanks to all of you who gave that answer. Now I have some confidence that I'm not as crazy as my husband thought!)

Getting off junk mail lists was the second most popular tip people gave for controlling the paper in their lives. I called the post office for information. The clerk gave me the following address and said to write a note saying you wanted off all mailing lists. Mail Preference Service, Direct Marketing Association, P O Box 9008, Farmingdale, NY 11735-9008. The clerk added, "Make sure you are specific. Write down the name of everyone in the household and your address. If you have moved in the last year, put that address down too."

Along with junk mail, magazines seemed to be a big problem for some people who were trying to control paper.

Dealing with magazines

Alicia wrote, "Then there's the magazine issue. Do you keep the whole magazine or just good articles? We only get six or so, but it doesn't take that long to get overrun with them."

Stop magazine subscriptions. This was the third most popular tip for controlling paper. However, if you have a hobby you might still want to get subscriptions. When you are finished with them, you can take them to friends, nursing homes, prisons, hospitals, doctors' offices, or the library. Find an outlet that is close to your home so you can drop off the magazines when you go do your grocery shopping. There's always the recycle bin if you can't find someone you can pass them on to.

My friend, Myra, says she has magazine holders. (She bought cardboard ones. However, you can buy plastic ones. My sister uses cereal boxes that she has cut.) Myra says she keeps her magazine holders on bookshelves. She places the magazines in them as soon as they come into the house. When she wants to look at a particular magazine, she knows right where to find it.

Many women said that as they read the magazines they take out the articles they want to keep. I found that when I did this, I didn't always file the articles right away, so another stack of work awaited me. When I did manage to file everything, I would have drawers of files and hardly ever look at them.

Finally I decided to keep only information that I really wanted at my fingertips, for example, interior decorating, gardening, and herbal remedies. I already had three-inch binders and plastic sheets that go into the binders. It only takes a minute for me to take an article out of a magazine and slip it into the plastic sheet. I don't have to punch holes into the article or glue it on to another sheet of paper. Another benefit of using the clear plastic sheets is that both the back and front of a page can be read. A friend said this wouldn't work in his situation. Here again, we need to use what works for us.

Whether we are trying to take care of our magazines or file other papers, the actual filing of the papers can be a problem.

Filing papers

"There is the whole filing question," Alicia said. "I keep looking for a good system that will serve me instead of me serving it. I feel that someday I could have a whole room of filing cabinets and never the time to look in any of the drawers."

It is sometimes difficult to decide what we will use, sometimes hard to make choices.

One person wrote that when he can't make choices, he throws things into a holding bin, and when he has time later, he makes a decision. Often the passage of time makes the decision easier. The problem with some of us is that our holding bins are sky high and we never find the time later.

Mona said that if she can remember her goals, then she doesn't have trouble deciding what she needs to keep.

I have an artist friend who collects a lot of pictures. She said, "I probably have enough to last ten years. I finally decided that if I could find them in a library, I didn't need to keep them myself. It cuts down on the clipping and filing and storing that I have to do."

For a quick filing of income tax receipts, Margie uses a large envelope with a magnet on it that is attached to her file cabinet. I throw income tax receipts into an empty five-pound laundry detergent box. Some people store all their records on the computer.

Here's a warning to all pet owners about filing their papers. Watch all the papers you have sitting around waiting to be filed. My sister just called saying her cat chewed on a piece of paper and dragged it into another room!

A friend, Chloe, laughingly told me another pet-and-paper story. She said, "My husband and I were gone for a few days. Papers to be filed were stacked in piles on our bedroom floor. Our adult children accidentally left the cat locked in our bedroom for three days. The cat used the papers on the floor for her bathroom. Now I try to file my papers more quickly!"

I found that I filed papers more quickly when our file cabinet was placed out in the dining room beside the kitchen counter. (The kitchen counter is where all the mail gets placed when we bring it into our home.) I could read, sort, and file the paper without leaving the room or putting the paper down. So my tip would be to put your filing cabinet, or whatever you use to file your papers, closest to where the papers get placed when you bring them into your home.

Other people gave additional hints on how to take control of the paper that comes into your life.

Additional tips for controlling paper
- Use recycled envelopes as scratch paper for lists and to keep score for games.
- Use the other side of used computer paper for scratch paper.
- Keep a spiral notebook by the phone for messages. You won't have small pieces of paper getting lost.

- Keep a small notebook in your purse and another in the car for the same reason.

For those of us who are inclined to be forgetful, Pat gave a tip. She said she keeps a list of everything she sends out and the date. She can quickly see if and when something was sent. It keeps her from having to look in each individual file folder or in a stack of papers waiting to be filed.

Irene said, "My tip is to never set it (paper) down. File it or toss it. If I don't, it becomes 'The Pile.' I have two paper piles right now. Both six inches deep!"

This wouldn't work in all situations; for example, if the mail comes when you have company. But, if we could make it a habit, don't you think Irene's tip would help us simplify our lives?

What about papers that have sentimental value like our son's first kindergarten picture, the hand print or hand outline of our first-grader, or the award that our child won in the geography bee?

When my son was in grade school a friend advised, "Pick one thing from each year and save it."

My sister added, "Don't stress out to keep something from every year. You might want to save two things from one year and nothing from another."

When choosing what to keep and what to throw away, you will probably throw away something that you might later wish you had kept and keep things that you could have thrown away. Don't feel guilty or get depressed over things. Remember it is the people and the memories that are important, not things.

We all need to do what works for our personalities and finances.

But there are things we all can do to partially control the paper blizzard that enters our lives.

Chapter 6

Stuffing Stuff

Some people's homes are like overstuffed Thanksgiving turkeys. They have stuff coming out the seams! No matter how much space they have, it still gets filled up.

My friend, Bonnie, sent this note. "I've started organizing my life, and it's a nightmare at the moment. I thought I was organized until I took the boxes of "stuff" out of our walk-in closet and started 'sorting.' At the end of my organizing session I had just looked through everything and put it back a bit neater than the way it was! That's silly!"

Many wives said it was easier to get rid of their husband's things than their own. Maybe they are like Peggy. She sent this e-mail, "Husband's 'stuff' is junk. Wife's is collectibles!"

My niece decided when she got married she only needed one set of dishes. Good for her.

She's already learning to keep things simple. However, sometimes we either need more dishes or need to use paper ones.

Once when my mother was visiting she was putting the clean

dishes away. "Don, where do all these glasses go?" she asked my husband.

"I don't know," he answered, "we've never had that many all clean at one time."

Teri is a younger person who has already made some wise decisions. She has only been married for seven years but she says, "My husband and I have come to the realization we don't need more money to buy more things and then more money to maintain them. If we don't have the time and energy to look after things, then it is wiser not to have them. We try to make good choices about how much 'stuff' we need to make us happy. For example, if we already have five tablecloths, do I need to go out and buy numbers six or seven? Life is already run, run, run. We need to stop the merry-go-round before it starts. I've decided to keep only my favorite things and give the others away to someone who can use them—family, friends or charity."

Maybe we all should adopt Teri's philosophy.

On a recent trip I saw the road sign, "$500 Throw Away Penalty." "Hmm," I thought, "Would we buy more 'stuff' if every time we bought something, we had to pay a $500 penalty to get rid of something we already owned?"

Here are some of the other ideas women shared on how they control "stuff" in their homes:

- You have to be firm with yourself about what you keep and what you throw away.
- Being organized helps. Get it before it gets you!
- Gradually learn priorities and get rid of what you don't use.
- Have a place for everything and everything in its place.
- Every once in a while when you are in a "get rid of" mood, pick one area and get rid of the excess.
- Recycle everything—paper, glass, cardboard, magazines.
- Put things in boxes and store in garage or a designated storage spot. If you haven't used it in a couple of years, out it goes! (This

was the number one answer to how people controlled the "stuff" in their lives.)

- Every time a charity calls, try to give them something.
- Rotate your decorations. Put some things out for a while and pack the rest away. When you feel like a change, switch. (Many women did this. Just so long as you don't want a change every day!)

Melba disagrees with some of the above suggestions. She said, "This year I really simplified my life. I cleaned out everything I didn't need and haven't used. I didn't try to recycle anything. I just hauled everything to a charity. I didn't want to take the energy to deal with recycling or a garage sale."

There are also different opinions on garage sales. Connie said, "Don't go to garage sales!" Minnie agrees, "If I can stay away from garage sales, I can control the 'stuff' in my life!"

However, Donna says, "I buy a lot of our games and children's toys at garage sales. I have one or two garage sales a year to get rid of excess 'stuff' in my house."

Maybe we can take Jean's advice, "I'm going to encourage my favorite charity to have a garage sale to raise money and help my friends and myself to get rid of things we don't want. The trick will be to bring home less 'stuff' than we took!"

You can see every woman needs to do what fits her personality, time, and energy level. She doesn't need to feel as if she has to do things like somebody else does unless it will work in her situation.

My friend Roni said that when she and her brother were small, their mom would only allow them five toys out at a time. The rest she put away. She allowed them to play with those toys for three weeks. She then put those toys away and put different ones out. "It helped us keep our rooms neat. It also kept us entertained because it was like we were getting new toys every three weeks," she said.

In all this getting rid of "stuff," let's remember we don't want to throw away our past to simplify our future. If we have something of sentimental value, we will want to keep it.

When I decorated our bedroom, I decided that the only things I wanted on our walls were the things that meant something to us. I didn't want to buy pictures just to have something on the walls that went with our color scheme.

I looked at what I already had. My mom had saved one of my first dresses and the wooden hanger that it had hung on. There was a picture of me wearing the dress. I also had a little silver fork and spoon I had used as a toddler.

What could I do? Out of all the display possibilities, I chose to have a shadow box made. It now hangs on a wall in our bedroom. I am happy that I rescued those treasures from a drawer. I can enjoy looking at them every day instead of only when I would look through the "stuff" I have stored away. I'm glad my mother kept those things for me. I'm glad that in all the moves we made and the getting-rid-of-clutter binges that I go on, I hadn't thrown those things out.

Whatever we get rid of is a personal choice, and we don't need to compare ourselves to anyone else. We need to be comfortable with how we live. This is our goal for simplifying.

Chapter 7

The Money Game

"If I could get a handle on our finances it would simplify my life," Joan said.

Hallie, who has a "handle" on her finances, agrees. She says, "There is such freedom in not owing anything and being in control of my finances. Young people should be taught not to go into debt. They should be taught there is no peace or freedom in straining financially to keep up with their family, friends, or neighbors."

She must be right. Just this week a friend of mine said, "I'm so depressed and scared. I don't know how I'm going to pay all my bills.

"Every time I get a five-cent raise, I get a ten-cent bill!" Carlee moaned.

Finances seemed to be the number one priority for a lot of people when asked what they wanted to simplify the most.

I asked Jenny, who is a financial counselor, "What are the worst mistakes people make in dealing with their finances?"

Jenny replied, "Lack of a budget, lack of a plan, and lack of knowledge. People need financial goals. How many people say to their spouse, 'Honey, I hope you don't make so much next year. We really don't need so much money'? Some people think that having wealth is bad because money becomes a god. It can be just as much of a god if we are worrying about it all the time. Money only makes you more of what you already are."

Here are Jenny's recommendations for helping you to attain financial security:

- Make a budget—take a class if you have to. It might not seem like you are simplifying your life, but in the long run it will save you hours of time and energy.
- Set goals—short- and long-term goals, for example, not only for buying a house or a car but for retirement.
- Acquire knowledge—use a variety of ways—books, seminars, magazines.

Many people agreed with Jenny. They said what helped them the most was making a budget. Here were some ways they said they worked with a budget:

- Made the budget out for the year with specific payments to be made from each paycheck.
- Listed all of their bills. As they paid their bills, they changed the balance on what they owed.
- Kept both the interest rate and the dollars they spent on interest each billing cycle. They kept this with the balance they owed for that bill. They said seeing how much they would pay for interest helped to keep them from using their credit cards.
- Made a paper chain. The person that told me this said she had each link represent a hundred dollars that she owed. As each hundred dollars got paid off, she cut out the link. This kept her

on track as she saw the chain shrink.

- Set goals. Many kept pictures representing their goals on their refrigerators where they could see them every day.

Dereck, a CPA, says one of the biggest problems people have is not looking at what they are doing with their money or what they have actually done with it. They don't know "specifically" where all their money goes. His advice was to track all the checks for the past year. A person could just put all their checks for the past year on the table and sort them. He suggested a computer software program for keeping track of all of them. He also recommended only carrying around one credit card with a low credit line, such as five hundred dollars.

If you do use a computer to keep financial records, be sure to protect them with a password. That way if someone steals or otherwise gets access to your computer, they won't be able to use any of your accounts or other information.

Some other thoughts that were expressed about finances include:

- Move to a small town where everything is close by. The house and power are often cheaper in small towns too.
- We need to learn to barter. Bartering is trading one thing that you do or have for another thing you need that someone else does or has. (Interesting concept.)
- Make sure before you get married that you are not in debt! This came from a young couple who said, "Now we are young and in love and want to travel, but we can't because we were in debt when we got married and can't seem to get to the end of paying off our bills." (All you single ones out there take heed. It is too late for the rest of us!)
- Give up your car. It saves car payments, license fee, insurance, and it saves in a lot of other ways too. An important one is that you won't shop as much.

- If you try to save money by doing it yourself, it can cost more in the long run. If you don't have the skill or tools, you probably would be better off paying a professional to start with.
- Cut up your credit cards. One person said she did this and it was scary but gave her the feeling that she was finally trying to get control of her finances.

The process of paying bills was a problem for some. Others gave suggestions on how to make the process work more smoothly for you:

- Pay your bills together. Both of you will know what is going on. (Bev's self-defense clamor. I'm not responsible for anything that might happen if you do this!)
- Check your phone bills to be sure you're not paying for someone else's calls. You may find someone else's added to yours. You may find that you are being charged for a service you aren't using so you will be able to drop it.
- Use a basket or container for bills that come into the house. (I use an empty three-pound detergent box. I like it because I can stand the bills up with the return address at the top. I can see without lifting the bill out where it originated from. It also saves me lifting each bill to find another. Once they are paid, I file them—well actually they're in a pile waiting to be filed!)
- Pay the smallest bill first, the next month put what you would have paid on that bill on the next bill.
- Pay off the bill with the highest interest first.
- Use a balance transfer option to move higher-interest debt to lower-interest accounts.
- Many banks now offer online bill-pay options that make it easy to pay bills without having to write out so many checks.

You can see from the above suggestions that people deal with their finances differently, according to their own personality, finances, and time frame. I hope some of their suggestions help you.

The biggest problem most people cited in getting a handle on their finances was just sitting down and working on it.

My suggestion is to break each chore into small parts and reward yourself for each piece done. Just start writing down your bills. A bound notebook worked better for me than loose paper. This also could be done on the computer, as Dereck suggested.

For example: Take fifteen minutes and collect all your bills if they are not already in one place. Stop! Reward yourself. (But don't reward yourself by generating another bill!) In the next session, list all your bills: when they are due and the interest rate you are paying on them. Stop! Reward yourself.

Start where you need to. Each one of us is at a different place and will use different methods. But the idea of only working for fifteen minutes isn't as overwhelming as saying, "I need a one- or two-hour time slot."

No quick fix

Quite a few people laughingly said winning a lottery would solve their money problems. But since they didn't buy tickets, I think they better try something else.

My husband and I paid off our debts and credit cards, and it really did help to get rid of stress.

However, there was still something missing. Still something that I felt I needed to do to really simplify my life as far as our finances go.

What I felt I needed to do to help my soul was to be able to help make our own choices. I wanted to understand more about mortgages, income tax, life insurance, savings, and investing. In order to do that, I took some classes. I am still learning, but I have started on a road that I wish I had started on in high school or college.

It is ironic that when the information will do us the most good, we are the busiest working and raising children so we don't take the time to learn what might help us. Maybe high schools and colleges should make financial management classes mandatory.

You could take a class (in a classroom, by correspondence, or on the computer). You might be able to find a good book to read on the subject. Whatever you choose, do it in such a way that you are not adding more stress to your life.

Won't it be a relief in heaven not to worry about finances!

Chapter 8

Don't Shoot Your Computer!

Just this week a man in a town near where I live shot his computer. Was he frustrated? Yes! Did it simplify his life to shoot his computer? No! In fact it complicated it. One of the bullets went into an adjoining apartment. He is facing a reckless endangerment charge after he figures out how to get out of the hospital where he was taken for a psychiatric evaluation.

I know how he feels. There have been many times I would have liked to do violence to my computer! It seems like when I'm in a hurry, it acts like a two-year-old—it has a mind of its own! My computer and I are *combatible*. We are definitely not *compatible*.

Instead of shooting the computer when it frustrates us, we need to see how we can use it, because it's often vital.

A friend said it simplifies her life not to let her husband use her computer. Another friend agrees. She says her husband will add or change a program, not tell her, and then go on a trip. When she goes to use the computer, things will have changed, and she won't be able to do anything. I firmly believe no-fault divorce might be changed to computer-fault divorce.

Bob said he uses his computer to simplify his life by using it to make spreadsheets for data for budgeting, goals, and time management.

"I use the computer on lots of writing projects," my friend Sonja said. "My tip is when using your computer to write anything you don't want to lose, be sure to make a backup. Don't try putting the computer in reverse and trying to drive it somewhere. Backup means to make a copy of what you have done on a disc, tape, or CD."

Sonja said, "I lost most of one big project when my computer crashed." Personally, I have never seen a computer crash. By *crash* I think computer buffs mean something happens to the data you have entered, and you can't get it back.

This afternoon my friend Jill called and said her computer had "locked up." I think *locked up* means nothing happens when you type and/or the mouse won't move. The mouse is not an animal. It is a small attachment to the computer that moves the pointer on the screen. Jill had to get special software from the software company to rescue her. She was almost finished with a mailing to 2,000 people. Project on hold!

It would make it a lot easier for some of us if computer terms made more sense. I wish software companies would hire me to write their programs—if I could understand the language, anyone could. However, the programs might not work. On second thought, they don't always work anyway.

As I write this chapter, the words "This program has performed an illegal operation and will be shut down" keep appearing on my screen, then the page goes blank. The program then disappears, and I have to restart it again.

A friend said he thought the words "illegal operation" meant that there might be underworld activities going on in the computer. He could be right! Everything that happens acts like a mystery—

you see part of what is going on but have to guess at the rest. Maybe it is the computer police shutting down my computer.

To me, the words "illegal operation" mean illegal surgery is being performed inside my computer. It sometimes frustrates me to the point of wanting to perform my own major surgery on the computer! Why can't the message say in plain English, "You don't have enough memory"? I could understand that, I really am quite good at forgetting things. However, I thought that was due to my gray hair and the computer in my brain, not the computer on my desk.

Another phrase I think is a little difficult to comprehend is "cannot initiate port." I'm working with the computer (or at least trying to), not working on a boat! I guess I need to do what Becky said she did.

Becky took a computer course, and it simplified her computer use. Knowing how to use something makes a huge difference. Another friend said she read books that helped her. A third friend always reads the manual. That might help.

Ask others to help you with your computer problems. Many times others, like my husband, son, or friends, have quickly solved computer problems for me.

Several ladies said the use of e-mail really simplified their lives. It was better than using the phone because they could answer at their own convenience. Others like it because it is quicker than regular (snail) mail. Quicker to write, quicker to send, and quicker to get a response. That is, if it doesn't get lost in cyberspace like mine does every once in a while. (E-mail is electronic mail, a method of sending messages by using the computer and the Internet. It can be a real blessing.)

Some hints people gave me for using e-mail:

- Don't bother with salutations.
- Make it short and on only one subject so the person can respond right away.
- If you use e-mail for work and personal purposes, use two

different e-mail addresses. This will at least separate business
and personal e-mail. Some people may even benefit by using
more than two.

- Respond right away. One person suggested when you get e-mail,
give yourself three choices: file, delete, or forward. Otherwise it
will clutter your hard drive, snarl your software, or languish in
Limbo waiting for you to get back to it.

- Set up your e-mail program to automatically copy what you
send. Jake said, "If I have to refer to it, I have it. Every so often
I go in and delete the things on this file so I don't overload my
electronic file cabinet."

When asked what modern convenience simplified their lives
the most, some people actually energetically praised the computer.
Others touted e-mail. Still others have given up computers to
simplify their lives.

I like to use the computer to keep in contact with my friends. I
have three friends who live in different parts of the country. We
have started using the computer for a group chat once a week.

When you can use your computer to simplify your life, you
won't want to shoot it.

Chapter 9

Harried Homemaker

Are you a harried homemaker? Are you like Maria whose domestic interests are on the bottom of her list? Maria said, "I was taking a class in psychological measurements. As students we had to take all the tests that someday we might have to administer and interpret. One test was an interest inventory. When my results came back, 'domestic interest' was literally at the bottom of the list—the lowest possible score it could be. My husband's comment, when I showed him, 'It figures.' "

There are a number of us whose test results would be like Maria's. I was surprised to find that about one-fifth of all the women I interviewed were honest enough to say that they simplified housework by not doing it!

Single, married, divorced, widowed, it doesn't matter. There will always be housework. What can we do to simplify it?

In over two hundred responses I received to my questions, almost everyone had at least one comment about housework. What interested me when I interviewed women was what they actually *did*, what worked for them. Often more than one person gave the same suggestion. Some women gave hints that are opposite to hints that other women gave. This shows that some hints will work best for some people while opposite hints will work best for others. Of course, a number of factors affect what works for different people. These include attitude, the number of people living in the house, and schedules. Here are some of the tips I received:

- Do what you can do when you can do it and don't worry about the rest.
- Don't be concerned with being the perfect housekeeper.
- Shut the doors to every room in the house and have one clean where you can invite guests or enjoy yourself.
- Keep your house clean. It will look good, and you will feel good.
- Pay a housekeeper to come in and do the housework.
- Try putting objects away as soon as you finish using them. (For some of us, if we put objects away as soon as we finished using them, they would disintegrate from the shock.)
- Get rid of most of your knickknacks so the dusting goes faster.
- Get rid of some furniture so you won't have as much to take care of.
- Take your shoes off at the door. (This was a very popular hint.)
- Delegate tasks to each family member, including your husband. (My husband says you should only delegate tasks to your husband if you get his permission first.)
- Teach your children to pick up after themselves.
- Let children close their doors.
- Have certain days or certain times of the day to do certain jobs.
- Don't do the housework unless company is coming. (Who are you trying to impress, and why are you trying to impress them?)
- Only do the housework after company has gone. (If they see your housework needs doing, maybe they will volunteer to help.)
- Take a couple of hours and go through the house doing everything at one time. You are free the rest of the week.

- Break jobs into small tasks.
- Rotate what you clean. It might not all be clean at one time, but it eventually all gets done.
- Do one room a day. (Some people would rather do all the bathrooms one day or all parts of the bedrooms another. They need to do whatever is easiest for them to do.)
- Dust only the coffee table. That's what most people notice anyway.
- Try to keep clutter picked up. If a room is free of clutter, it can still need dusting or other work, but you won't notice it as much.
- Have different baskets for different colored laundry. Leave the baskets in the hall, where everyone can put dirty clothes or linens. It saves sorting before doing the wash.
- Simplify the laundry by throwing it out the window. (This from a man!)
- Dust bedroom with towels on their way to the laundry.
- Work from a list and cross the steps off after you have done them. This will give you a sense of accomplishment even if you don't get everything done on your list.

Most of these suggestions are not specific. There are times however, that we might need to follow specific housekeeping guidelines. There are times when doing housework will be a necessity. One of those times is if someone in your home has severe allergies or asthma. You might have to do several things to simplify your life. A recent news report featured an environmentalist telling how to help people with allergies. Here are some of her tips:

- Clean by vacuuming.
- Dust with a damp cloth.
- Take shoes off at the door.
- Wash sheets in hot water.
- Take out carpets.
- Cover pillows and mattresses with special cases that prevent dust

mites from contact with people.
- Don't smoke.
- Don't use fireplaces and wood stoves.
- Use electric heat.
- Use good furnace filters and keep them well-maintained.
- Make sure you have a good supply of fresh air.

It might seem like doing all the above would complicate your life. However, if it helps someone in your house to breathe easier, take less medication, and make fewer trips to the doctor, your life will be simplified.

Remember, not everyone will choose to do housework the same way.

"Why wash my walls?" one friend says, "I just have them painted every two or three years."

Another friend says, "Just the thought of painting almost lands me in the hospital! I pay someone to come and scrub my walls."

Kim says one time she chose not to do housework. She states, "My daughter had been sick, and I was busy taking her back and forth to the hospital and doctor. My house was a mess. I was knee-deep in dirty dishes and laundry when the school principal unexpectedly dropped by to see how my daughter was doing.

"He took one look at the mess and said, 'I'm glad to see you are human too!' "

There will always be housework, but maybe the realization that we are all human will help you know what to simplify in your situation. Simplify it to your own standards and not to someone else's. Not your mother's, not your sister's, not your neighbor's but your own standards. If a picture-perfect house is your daily goal, you can spend all your time cleaning. However, if you are like Maria and domestic interests are at the bottom of your list, you can just do what you need to do to survive. Whatever you choose, if it is your way, it will reduce the chances of you being a harried homemaker.

Chapter 10

Spare the Cook

Most cooks need to be spared work while some cooks may need to be spared embarrassment. Maryanne watched as the boy who was her special friend struggled to eat the lasagna on his plate. He tried to cut bite-size pieces with his fork. He couldn't. Next, he used a knife to help cut the lasagna. He couldn't. He studied the lasagna closely. His face twisted with a puzzled look as he pushed his fingers into his food on his plate. Maryanne nearly fainted with embarrassment as he pulled out paper from the middle of his lasagna. Her mother, while preparing the lasagna, had unwittingly put two slices of cheese stuck together trapping the paper between the pieces.

Could Barbara have been spared cooking embarrassment too? Barbara made chicken gravy, but she thought it was a little too pale. In trying to figure out how to make it darker, she remembered that green and red made brown. She grabbed the green food coloring and dumped some into the gravy. When she reached for the red food coloring, she discovered there wasn't any. So she served green gravy. The human eye is connected to the taste buds! Everyone refused to eat the green gravy even though it was perfectly good food.

Some people spare themselves embarrassment by refusing to cook at all. One woman put it this way, "I let my hubby do the cooking."

Some people like to cook—others do not. A person should not be judged by how they cook. But it might simplify their lives if they knew how to use a can opener!

So how can we simplify cooking without exposing ourselves to embarrassment? Here are cooking tips others use. Many gave the same tips, and I've listed them under various categories.

Simplify grocery shopping

Most people felt that shopping was one area of cooking that could really be simplified. Here are the suggestions they gave:

- Buy in bulk to save trips to the store. (Be careful how much bulk you are buying and lifting, or you may have to make trips to your physician while saving on trips to the store!)
- Buy everything at the first of the month but the fresh foods and make weekly trips to the store for them.
- Keep a shopping checklist on the refrigerator or a bulletin board so anyone in the family can add to it.
- Shop for groceries after you have had a good meal. (Hunger attacks in grocery stores can be damaging to your health and your pocket book. Those candy bins near the cash registers are for adults as well as children, and some desserts are just waiting for a hungry shopper to grab them. In fact, some days I think they have reached out and grabbed me!)
- Stick to one store. You will learn what is in each aisle.
- Write your shopping list according to what is in each aisle. This saves you from backtracking.
- If you shop in aisle order, your groceries will be easy to put away; for example, all frozen food together and all fresh vegetables together.

- Stick to your list and your budget.
- Each time you go into the store, enter through the same door.
- Try to keep a spare of everything, and when you start on the spare, you can add it to your list.
- Use coupons only for brands you regularly use or if using the coupon makes the product cheaper than your regular brand.
- Go alone. Don't take husband or children. Others said to take your husband because he can do the lifting. (To be fair, there are husbands who are good grocery shoppers. I know. I have one.)
- If you are unable to go to the grocery store, some grocery stores will deliver.

Using recipes and menus

There were conflicting ideas on whether using menus and recipes actually would simplify your life. I think this is where a cook's personality and cooking talents really are revealed. Do any of the following hints sound like what you do? Which ones are you the most likely to use and why? When you discover what works the best for you, you will have simplified your life:

- Don't make menus. Cook what you feel like cooking.
- Make menus and stick to them so you don't have to worry about what to fix.
- Standardize meals and have a day for each cooking job.
- Making menus helps you know what to put on your shopping list.
- Stick to recipes with few ingredients, steps, and utensils.
- Skip all recipes—it's too much trouble to dig them out.

Simplify your cooking

Here again is where you need to take into consideration your own personality. But this time you will also want to consider the energy and time you have before selecting one of the following ways to simplify your cooking:

- Cook with your children—this might not simplify your work at the moment, but it might simplify a relationship.
- Delegate jobs to your teenager or your husband.
- Do most of your own baking and cooking.

Use machines to simplify your cooking

Anytime you find a machine that helps you simplify your cooking and will save you time and energy, use it. But you also need to consider the time and effort it takes to care for the machine. If caring for a machine takes a great deal of your time or energy, it might not be worth the time it saves you.

Sometimes I have borrowed a machine from a friend to see whether I will really use it, but usually I prefer to help them use one at their home. This saves me from the chance of having to replace it if something happens to it.

Two machines people said really helped to simplify their cooking were the bread machine and the microwave. I was surprised at the number of people who said the microwave was the modern convenience they used the most.

Simplify your cooking by modifying foods

With more and more women working outside the home, cooking from scratch is no longer the symbol of the "perfect" cook like it used to be. The need for doing thinks more quickly and with less hassle is shown by the fact that quite a few who responded to my questionnaire said to buy prepared foods and modify them by adding ingredients. They gave examples like buying prepared spaghetti or chili and adding favorite ingredients.

Simplify by using cooking tricks

By using simple cooking tricks, you can simplify your cooking. Here are some of the tricks some cooks gave to help you:

- Get out all the ingredients and equipment you will need before you start to cook.
- When you have bought nuts, chop all of them at one time and store them in containers in the freezer.
- When chopping vegetables, do a large batch, freezing what you don't need immediately in small quantities. (When we were first married, I did this with fifty pounds of onions. Our small apartment had a rather strong smell for a few days. However, I had onions to use in recipes for the whole year. Right in the middle of chopping the onions, my husband's two elderly aunts unexpectedly came to stay for a couple of days. They appreciated the aroma too.)
- Hide the chocolate chips so you will have some to make chocolate-chip cookies.
- Place grains and dry foods in canning jars and leave them on your counter so they will be handy to use when needed.
- When guests are arriving and you don't have food prepared, sauté some onions. Do this even if you aren't going to use them in your cooking, so your guests will smell the aroma of onions and think dinner is almost ready. (This works for husbands too!)

Simplify making food last

Some cooks said that the best way to simplify cooking is to make food last:

- Cook double or triple batches. Then freeze the extra food for later use. (This was the most common technique people used to simplify their cooking. If you don't have the time or energy to do all the steps at once, break down making the recipe into small parts. For example, make the bread crumbs at a different time or mix all the dry ingredients and cover until you can finish the recipe. You still will be saving on dishes and energy.)
- Cook simple recipes in large enough quantities that last several days. Just warm up what you need each subsequent day putting

in different additional ingredients each day.

- Make cupcakes instead of cake if you live alone. (I must mention, however, that my friend Goldie disagrees. "I make a whole cake," she says. "I don't worry. I can eat it all myself. It's obvious when you look at me." By the way, Goldie is not her real name because she promised if I used her real name and she ever wrote a book, I'd be disgraced in it!)

- Make cookies when no one else is at home so you will have some when you get done. (You have to save them from the two-legged sugar pests that are lurking in your home. If one of those pests is the cook herself, you are in trouble!)

Eliminating foods to simplify

By eating plainer foods, the cook's work can be simplified. Here are a couple of tips that women gave to eliminate some of the cooking you would have to do:

- Eat fresh fruits and vegetables in their raw state to avoid cooking.
- Skip desserts.

Some people felt that the prize tip came from the woman who said, "If worst comes to worst eliminate cooking altogether and eat out!"

I appreciate all the tips that were given to me. If you have more that you would like to share with me, please send them to one of the addresses listed in chapter 1.

Sometimes having other people cook for you may not simplify your life. Shirley asked her son to cook the spaghetti for supper. When she came into the kitchen, she saw spaghetti on the ceiling, spaghetti on the walls, spaghetti everywhere. Her son had heard spaghetti would stick to the wall when it was cooked. He had been testing it.

It is becoming quite popular for four or more ladies to form a co-op and just cook one night a week for all the families in the co-op. If families have the same tastes and no allergies, it could work.

Cooking for others would not simplify my life even if it was for only one night a week!

That is the way the Lord made us. All different. We need to simplify our cooking by choosing what is easiest for us.

Chapter 11

Lunch On the Run

We were eating on the run. We didn't have time to go home and cook. Burritos supreme sounded good. We stopped at a fast food restaurant. At the drive-up window, Don, my husband, was doing the ordering. The rest of us were giving our preferences. Some wanted onions, some did not. Some wanted hot sauce, some did not. We all wanted bean burritos. The poor girl taking the order must have been confused. Don paid the cashier and took the bag. After we had driven away, we got out the burritos and started to eat. Then we started to compare our burritos. Some burritos had hot sauce. Some did not. Some had onions. Some did not. None of us had beans in our burritos. We all had just one other thing in our burritos—lettuce. The girl who took the order must have thought, "What a funny group of vegetarians!"

When asked what they did about eating away from home, some people said they always take their own lunches. Others like to eat at restaurants. It depended on their financial situations, personalities, and how they used their time.

Here are some hints from several people on what they did when taking their food with them:

- Always keep water and bite-sized foods in the car.
- Keep a basket containing paper plates, cups, bowls, plastic utensils, paper towels, and wet wipes in your car. All you have to do is stop at a store to buy food, and you are ready to eat.
- Keep a pocketknife in the car.
- Take a cucumber—it freshens up any meal.
- Make a pot of chili or polenta or soup. Take the whole pot in the car. There are zippered carrying bags that will keep food hot or cold.
- Carry peanut butter, fruits, and vegetables—then buy the bread.
- Even when just out shopping, pack a lunch—it saves money and time.

Others said that it was too much of a hassle to take their food with them. Eating at restaurants seemed simpler. They liked the idea of no preparation and no cleanup. They felt that they could relax more if they took the time to eat in a restaurant. Here are the tips that those people who like to eat in restaurants gave:

- Eat a la carte—you can usually get more of what you want.
- Eat at salad bars or buffets—probably the most popular tip— each person in a group can usually find something they like.
- Be specific and clear about what you want.

You might like to eat at a fancy restaurant sometimes, just for the enjoyment. If you have busy workdays away from home, you might like to pack a lunch or buy one at a deli and go to a park or somewhere outside to eat. If you can't get away from your desk or if you have to eat in a lunchroom and need a break, you could take a cassette and listen to soft, relaxing music through headphones. Tell people you are taking a class. You are. You are taking a class in relaxation!

Many people said that they like to travel and spend a lot of time away from home. Here are some of the ways they made eating on the run easier for themselves:

- When traveling we like to stop at motels where we can have kitchenettes so we can cook our own food.
- Once when we went on a trip, I packed all the lunches and labeled them. All we had to do was buy fruit. As the food was eaten, we had a place to put souvenirs.
- We like to eat our main meal at restaurants at noon. It is cheaper than eating dinner at restaurants. At night we can relax and eat in our room.
- A good friend made us granola to take on a trip. It was delicious and practical. We just had to add fresh or canned fruit and had a good breakfast that lasted us until lunchtime. It was quick to use because she had put it in self-sealing plastic storage bags. We used paper cups and plastic spoons, so there was no cleanup.

You might choose to take your lunch or to buy it at a restaurant. Whatever works best for you will simplify your life.

Chapter 12

To Preserve or Not to Perserve

In this chapter we are talking about preserving food, not preserving bodies over fifty!

A large number of women said they used to can and freeze food but no longer do it. They don't have the time, the energy, or a garden.

The women who preserve food gave these tips:

- Work with at least one other person. It can be a social time as well as a preserving time. (I was surprised to find this was the number one tip for preserving food.)
- Only preserve food you will eat and enjoy.
- Buy a ten-pound can of applesauce and freeze the sauce in individual size containers. These are good for taking in lunches or for people eating or living alone.
- For freezing runny stuff: Put a freezer bag into an empty cottage cheese carton. Put the top edge of the freezer bag over the sides

of the carton. Fill with the food, then seal the bag.
- For canning pears and peaches, add a heaping tablespoon of pineapple juice concentrate to your pitcher of syrup.

Betty, who has severe health problems, says, "I used to can and freeze every piece of garden produce I could grow or pick. Now, I have discovered it is OK if I don't do anything. I can also take shortcuts. For example, this year instead of picking strawberries, which I can no longer do, I bought a large bucket of strawberries already picked, washed, and sliced. I just put them into freezer bags and added a small amount of sugar."

"Bev," Betty said, "be sure to tell people that whether they preserve food or not should have nothing to do with their self-esteem. Somehow when I was growing up, I got the message that I needed to preserve food if I was going to be the perfect woman."

This year a friend canned and froze a lot of produce. She felt she had to do it because she is a diabetic. She had to take three days off work because she was so tired. Was it worth it?

If there is something special you or your family like to have preserved at home, such as frozen berries, make it a family affair. Take the whole family to pick the berries. Have them help do the preserving. Of course, this could be a hassle if your children are young. If it is too much of a hassle, don't do it. Just remember you will build memories as well as preserve food. (Sometimes you might think you can do without the memories!) If you live alone, ask friends to go with you.

Sometimes there is someone in the family who really likes a special food preserved and you don't feel like taking the energy or time to do it. Get the person who likes the preserved food to do the work or help with the work. He or she might decide they don't like it as much as they thought, and you won't feel guilty when you don't do the preserving.

Each person must decide for herself whether she is going to

preserve food. Jolene says, "I buy everything on sale for almost the same price I would pay if I were to can or freeze it. Why waste my time and energy?"

Rosemarie says, "I don't care about the price. I like to can and freeze fruits and vegetables so I can make sure I'm getting top produce."

Do what is easiest for you. Don't compare yourself to your sister, mother, or grandmother!

If we wear ourselves out trying to preserve food, it will be our bodies that will need the preserving!

Chapter 13

Taming Your Time

Taming your time can be like a dog trying to catch its tail. You never quite make it.

Have you ever thought about what would help you control your time the most? When people talked about controlling their time, the five most often-mentioned things were:

- Get rid of the television.
- Don't answer the phone.
- Use a schedule—write down daily goals.
- Use lists—cross off things as you do them because this gives you a sense of accomplishment.
- Use your computer to keep track of your schedule. Every day your schedule will show up on the screen. You can even get reminders the day before.

My husband uses his computer to remind him of important

things. He put my mother's birth date in the computer. He wanted the date to show up the day before her birthday. It showed up every day for a month. Every day he was reminded that the next day would be her birthday. We figured she was either aging awfully fast or there was a bug in the program.

Lucia advised, "Plan some flex time. In other words, allow for the unexpected."

"I do best when I set realistic time frames for doing each job," Denise said.

"The only way I will get control of my time is by having a dictator around to make me do it," Lottie laughed.

"My daily planner is very useful and simplifies my life a lot. It helps me plan my time. I have used it for many years. A friend who was an office manager used one and got me started. My daily planner is a loose-leaf notebook with a page for each week. Each page is divided into the days of the week. Even though I don't work outside my home, I use mine constantly. I use it to write down any projects I need to work on, physicians' appointments, or meetings of the organizations I belong to," Mavis said.

A number of people felt if they were better organized, they could control their time. They felt being organized meant they had every minute scheduled. This included when they were riding in the car, standing in a line, waiting in a dentist's or doctor's office. They thought they should always have a book to read, a notebook to write in, or something to listen to.

One friend said, "I worked hard for a number of days. Then one day I had nothing planned. I felt guilty all day, as if I should be doing something."

In business, companies sometimes schedule "down" time for their equipment to be repaired. This is time when the equipment cannot be used. Maybe we need to start scheduling down time for our bodies. Time when we will be rejuvenated: vacation time, tea time, time for exercise, time to be alone if we are with people all the time, time to be with people if we are alone most of the time, time for a date with our spouse or children, time for a walk on the beach, time to watch a sunset, time for a hobby, time to do whatever would help us enjoy life more. But perhaps most of all, we might need to learn to be able to sit in a chair and do nothing.

Maybe we need to tell ourselves it is OK to stand in line and do nothing. If we need to take our mind off the one-hour commute to the office, why not listen to tapes that make us laugh and relax instead of tapes that are trying to teach us something?

What would happen if we said we were going to put less things on our "to do" list? If you are spinning like the dog trying to catch its tail, find something to stop that spinning. Start by taking fifteen minutes a day and doing nothing.

Chapter 14

When Adult Children Come Home to Roost

Like chickens coming back to the henhouse to roost for the evening, more and more adult children are coming home for extended periods. Sometimes they bring spouses, children, and pets with them.

What happens when adult children come home for a while? Here in their own words are what actually happened to some people.

Darselle's married son and his wife and three children came home for three months. "I was still working, so I retreated to my bedroom and let them take over the house and the kitchen. I tried to make it safe to communicate. I tried not to make a big deal of breakage. [Good idea with three small children!] I'm sure my daughter-in-law was glad to see me go to work each day. At the end of the three months my son said, 'Mom, I didn't think you and Dad would make it!' "

"Don't do it if it is not absolutely essential. It was a real mixed bag. My grandson was the prize!" Ruth said.

One friend honestly said that after a few weeks the tension was too much. She said, "Yes, I let them stay one week, two weeks, three weeks. I wrote them a note and left it on their pillow. If you stay one more week, you'll need to pay a month's rent. They left."

Jacey said, "My daughter and her husband, who are in their late teens, came home for a month. They wanted to be independent. When they were working, they asked me to make phone calls for them. When they got home, I would give them the messages. Then they would get angry. I finally told them I would not make any more calls for them."

There was conflict in Tom's family too. Tom said, "My daughter and her husband came home too. They are in their late twenties. They didn't have a car and expected to use ours any time they wanted. I work different shifts. They would expect me to get up and pick them up from work. When my wife and I would do things together, they would figure I should be sleeping! It was better for all of us when they finally moved into their home."

Over a three-year period, Paula had three different children come to live at home for a while. She said it depended on which child was home. "One child liked loud music and brought his dog. (I don't have animals in my house!) One child ate at all hours and didn't want to eat with the rest of us when we ate. The third child helps with the housework, and her hours are the same as mine. She is a joy to have around. I love all of my four children very much. But if having one or more visit doesn't make my day happier, it is best to have a short stay before anyone gets upset."

Gena's daughter has come home for six months. Gena said, "She thinks she is a guest and rarely cleans up."

When Jackie's nephew came to stay, he was lazy. "It was horrible! I didn't wait on him at all. I wasn't the heavenly host!" she said.

When my son, Ryan, was three years old, he and I spent two months with my folks while my husband looked for a job in another city. Ryan behaved quite well, until we were to leave on the plane to rejoin Don. Just before we were to leave, Ryan took a black felt permanent marker and made a zigzag mark all down my folks' carpeted stairs that went from the living room to the basement. I know they were glad to see us get on that plane!

Ben laughed, "My daughter and son-in-law were living with us. They went to visit my friend Chuck. Chuck said to my son-in-law, 'If you can make it through all the things that have happened to you in the past six months, you will be doing great.' My son-in-law replied, 'If we can make it through living with my in-laws it will be a miracle.' "

Ben said, "I thought it was funny because I felt the same way when we had to stay with my in-laws for a couple of months."

Different situations call for different solutions. Here is the advice some people gave on how to simplify living with adult children:

- Remember that adult children are friends, not children. Esther said she didn't lay down any rules, but they had agreed-upon principles that helped them live in harmony: "I don't have rules for my adult friends, so why have them for my children? We are all adults. We were all working, so we shared household chores. Everyone was responsible for cooking one meal during the week. When friends stay with you, they let you know when they expect to be back. They call if something changes. I expected my adult children to do the same."
- Others said rules are important. They said to give your adult children your love and support but to have rules and spell them out.
- Learn to *cluck, cluck*. Listen but not give advice.
- Just enjoy the time you have together.
- Put them to work!
- Keep out of each other's business. They shouldn't know yours anymore than you know theirs.

Chet said, "You'll always love your children. But that doesn't mean you have to love having them live with you. Just keep saying to yourself, 'This too shall pass.' "

Other people loved having their children live with them. Each situation was different.

Chapter 15

Take Time for Tea

"When I need a break," Karili said, "I go out on the dock on the small pond behind our house and have a cup of tea."

We don't all have a small pond behind our homes, but we all can take tea breaks.

Why tea? Because drinking tea signifies a resting, a pause in the frantic rush through our day. Because we all need breaks in our day. Because the thought of drinking tea usually brings thoughts of getting a calmer response than drinking coffee.

In other words, if you need to put a calming break in your day, you might have a tea break. If taking a tea break would stress you out because it would be just another thing "to do," then don't take one. If you are lonely, you might want to ask a friend over for tea or have a tea party as a way to mingle with people. You have to decide what is best for you. I challenge you, just once, try a tea break.

My sister says, for her, drinking tea is a taste of long ago. It is a retreat into a different time. A time when things were slower. She says the real tea break is a lingering over, a sipping of the tea.

Others must agree with her. The number of tea houses or tea shops in the metropolitan area where I live has doubled in the past year and a half.

Everyone needs periods of time when they can recharge their body and mind. Attending a tea party to some would recharge their soul. To others it would complicate their lives.

Use a tea break to strengthen you when:

- You are lonesome or just needing to talk with someone—call a friend to come for tea. You could call someone you don't know very well and make a new friend.
- You are needing to take a pause in your mad dash through the day, whether at home or on the job.
- You are going through a crisis in your life.
- You need to be alone.
- You want to celebrate with friends—have a tea party. A tea party is different than a regular party because it suggests getting together not for games or excitement but for a bonding. For relaxation and talking. If you keep it simple and relaxed, it can be a great way to visit with friends and relax at the same time. Just a simple cup of tea doesn't cause the hostess or guests too much work or frustration.
- You want to make yourself feel special—attend a fancy tea. If you are the type of person who likes to have an occasion to put on your best clothes and go somewhere special, a fancy tea might be for you. You could call a friend to go with you. It wouldn't simplify your life in terms of cutting back. However, it might simplify your life in adding something that might put a sparkle in your eye or give you something to look forward to. It might give you a certain comfort in knowing you can do something special.
- You are traveling—tea to go. Take steeped tea in a thermos or

hot water in a thermos and tea bags. Just remember, if you drink too much tea when you are traveling, it will be you who is running and not the car.
- You want to make family time special or start a family tradition—once a month or to celebrate something special as a family.

Choose your tea. A quick visit to the grocery store will show you there are many different types of tea. There are many alternatives to teas with caffeine. You can choose fruit teas, herbal teas, or a combination of teas.

My friend Juliann says if you really want to make your tea break special, use a lovely china cup and saucer. Drinking from one makes her feel pampered.

If you want to take a tea break and don't have a pond to sit beside:

- Put a relaxing tape or CD on a portable player and listen while you have your tea.
- Soak in the tub in an herbal bath while sipping a soothing tea—from an unbreakable cup.

Having a tea party with guests would not simplify my life. But if having a tea party would give you pleasure, here are some hints:

- You could have a tea party to celebrate a special occasion or have an annual tea party as a gift to your friends—instead of giving them gifts any other time of the year. You can make a simple tea party or a fancy tea party. Make it easy on yourself.
- Use what you have. When Jerry had a tea party, she used her collection of china tea cups and plates. None of them matched. Yet it was elegant. If you don't have cups, have the guests bring their favorite tea cup or mug.
- You could have hot soapy water afterward so the guests could

wash their own cups.

- If you don't have a teapot, do you have a soup tureen? If a friend has a teapot, have her bring it and be in charge of making and taking care of the tea that is in her pot.
- Ask the guests to bring their favorite teas.
- You could provide the tea and have the guests bring sandwiches, fruit, or dessert. Or you could suggest no food, just tea.
- Guests do not have to sit at tables. However, if they will not be sitting at tables, make sure they have a place to put their cups. If you will be using several tables, the tablecloths do not have to match. You might even borrow some from your guests. You might ask a guest to be in charge of decorating the table. If you are using more than one table you could ask different people to be in charge of the different tables.
- Instead of tables, you could serve the tea from a coffee table, the top of a chest of drawers, or trays.
- Use your creativity, not your time or money to have your tea party—unless you have plenty of time and money and enjoy sharing.

For you, simplifying hosting a tea party might mean paying someone to come and help or taking your guests to a fancy restaurant or tea room. Do what fits your situation.

Maybe every woman should attend one fancy tea in her life.

Attending a fancy tea

You might go to a fancy hotel, to one of the many tea rooms that are opening around the country, be invited to a private tea party or attend your nearest college. Attending a fancy tea did not simplify my life. I'm one of those women who maybe should not have attended a fancy tea.

I attended a college associated with a hospital. A class on social etiquette was required for graduation. Students were required to attend the annual Christmas tea put on every year. It was hosted by the famous and wealthy main benefactor to the college and hospital. Our teacher made sure we understood that we were in no way to disgrace the college at this distinguished person's luxurious home.

I went with my roommate, Dee, who picked up her tea while I chose to get some cookies. There were some little, round, chocolate cookies on the top layer of a tiered cake plate. I picked up the tongs and squeezed a cookie. Whoops! It slipped. I tried again. And again. Round and round the cookie went. I'd squeeze the tongs and think I had a good grip. There it would go again.

I glanced over at Dee just in time to see her spill her tea from her cup into her saucer. I didn't dare look at her face. I was already doing what any self-respecting woman does when she doesn't know what to do and is under tension. Giggling. In this fancy home with a number of sophisticated people around, I didn't dare let the giggles out. I'm sure my face was red. I know I was shaking like a tower in an earthquake.

"Pick up the cookie with your fingers, dear," I heard whispered in my ear. I looked up to see the elegant mother of our hostess. She probably thought, *That girl is going to hold up this line all night if we don't get her out of here*—she was right; *that girl is a little out of her class*—she was right!

Dee and I finally managed to get our tea and cookies. We went into another room and let our hysterical giggles out. For some reason I haven't attended a fancy tea since.

No, that fancy tea did not simplify my life! But I have attended other teas which were much simpler and more relaxing.

Chapter 16

Daisy, You're Not Crazy

"I don't know what is the matter with me. I feel like I might be going crazy," Daisy sighed. "I don't want to get out of bed in the morning, I'm exhausted all the time, I feel depressed for no reason, and I don't know what I want to do. I want to do things for myself. Most days I wish I could be by myself. There are things I need to deal with, but I don't have the energy. Little things irritate me that at other times wouldn't bother me at all. It is awful to say, but sometimes I wish I wasn't even here."

Have you ever felt that way? Earlier this week, three different women have said the same thing. A number of women whom I interviewed said there have been times in their lives when they have felt the same way. What is going on? I am not talking about menopause. These feelings can come whenever we are dealing with major changes in our lives. Changes like dealing with a retired husband, dealing with a teenage child, dealing with losing a job, or dealing with a major illness. Men sometimes have these feelings too. However, women tend to be more willing than men to express them.

All through our lives things happen to us when we have to deal with changes. Sometimes we can sail right through them. The next time the very same incident will have us whirling like leaves in a windstorm.

Don't you think the way we react depends on our personalities? However, it also depends on our health and finances. Sometimes just being exhausted or "burdened out" can make us have the same symptoms.

Darlene said, "Just knowing others sometimes feel the same way relieves my mind. It doesn't make me happy to know that someone else is going through the same thing. But I don't feel so alone when I'm feeling this way."

When you are feeling like you might be going crazy, is it possible that simplifying your life in some way might help you deal with how you feel?

Delores, a nurse, has felt the same way Daisy is now feeling. She gave me these tips:

- See a physician and get a good physical exam. Delores learned that her thyroid medication needed adjusting. She said it is important to rule out a physical problem first.
- Admit you are having these feelings. It is OK to feel the way you do. Learn that it is OK to have negative feelings. It is how you act out those feelings that can be good or bad. If you can say, "I feel sad, mad, or depressed, you can go on and find out why and work on changing things."
- Talk to a friend. It can help you when someone says, "I have felt that way too."
- Take a break from your routine for a couple of days or a week or two. You probably have "burnout."

Here are hints others gave:

- Get some exercise. Just start to walk. If you can't go outside, do something inside. Walk in place while listening to music that has a beat to it.
- At the end of each day be thankful for at least one thing. Keep a record of things for which you are thankful.
- Keep a journal. Write down everything. Especially note how you feel or react to certain situations or food.
- Get information. If you are dealing with a career change or what to do with your life, see what talents you have. One lady said she went to her local community college. Her tests showed she'd be a good colonel in the army! She asked if she should go to an army recruiter and ask him if the army is taking women over fifty for colonels now!
- Do something for yourself. One friend who is going through feelings of anger says she feels like she's given and given until she can give no more. Spend money or time or energy on yourself. It can be something small like reading a book while relaxing in a hot tub. It can be something bigger like going away for a day, a weekend, or a week or two. A lot of women made these same suggestions.
- Consider professional counseling.
- Find something to laugh at. You'll feel better after you've had a good laugh. Find an old sitcom or movie or read a funny book.
- Pray about it. Many women said praying about how they felt sometimes helped give them a sense of peace.
- Take vitamin supplements. A number of women said they feel better when they take vitamin supplements. A news program I heard recently said that some doctors are now adding supplements to their treatment methods. Use discretion when taking any supplements.
- Find something to celebrate each day. This would be a little different than doing something for yourself as stated above. You would actually say, "Today I'm celebrating the first snowflake, the rainbow I saw, my birthday, or the bird's nest I saw this

morning." The point is to verbalize what you are celebrating to one other person. You might ask them to celebrate with you. If you can't leave home or have a friend in, how about sending a note to someone saying "Today I am celebrating ____." If you have a computer and have e-mail, send your note that way. What if you can't write a note? What about phoning? The point is to do whatever would be easiest and fun for you. Make it a simple celebration, something that might take fifteen minutes or less to prepare or do. Maybe just buying one carnation or other flower to keep or give away. Just celebrate something.

"Any one of these steps seems like it might add more to my life rather than simplifying it," Sheila said. "But I have found if I do even one of them, although it takes more time to start with, it actually can help me cope."

Remember, whatever you are feeling, Daisy, you will survive. One lady put it this way, "When you are going through changes or discouragement, don't give up."

Chapter 17

Rating the Dating

How do you rate your dating? Do you go on dates with your husband or, if you're single, with friends?

"A date? What's a date? Do people still go on dates? I don't remember the last time I went on a date!" wrote my single friend Jackie. Well, Jackie, there are a lot of married couples who could say the same thing.

One friend said, "Some husbands don't know what dates are." She added, "Don't use my name. He might find himself in there."

My dictionary says a date is "an appointment for a specified time."

Everyone needs to have appointments "for a specified time." If they are married, they need time alone with their spouse. If they are single, they need time to be with their friends.

How is planning dates going to simplify my life? If I'm already stressed out with things to do, one more thing is going to add to my stress, right? Wrong. It might be an extra thing to do, but it might be a simple pleasure that will keep you going all week.

Dates act like glue. They cement relationships. When my husband and I take turns planning a date, we are happier.

Here are some simple things people say they do for dates (Please note, Jackie, although most of these ideas came from married couples, most of them could be done with singles asking other singles to join them):

- Go for walks in the woods, mountains, or at the beach.
- Visit friends.
- Go on picnics. (Most popular answer for cheap dates.)
- Go camping.
- Once a month have a Saturday night get-together for friends. Include married and singles. Take turns having it at each other's homes. Don't think the homes have to be spotless. If someone doesn't have a big enough home, let them host it at someone else's house. Have everyone just bring one dish. The only dish that is hot is the dish the hostess serves. This simplifies use of the kitchen.
- Eat out at a restaurant for under $10 for both of you.
- Play miniature golf.
- Go bowling.
- Go to the library.
- Go window shopping in a mall and buy a small treat such as a cookie or doughnut.
- Take your own food and just drive around to areas you haven't seen before. The amount of money you have for gas determines how far you can go.
- Go to bookstores.
- Go to a fast food restaurant and just buy a hot drink, milkshake, or soft drink.
- Ride bikes.
- For singles, work with a group. One lady said she likes to work

with community service groups. She is with people, and it doesn't cost anything.

- Picnic in your home on the porch or in front of the fireplace if you can't go anywhere.
- Play tennis.
- Roller skate.
- Trade baby-sitting with a couple of other families with children.
- Go to free concerts in parks in the summer.
- Visit gardens together.
- Watch videos at home.

Maybe that last couple agrees with Laurie who wrote, "You can have enjoyment doing anything as long as it's together and not stressed or hurried."

Mindy said, "The more we do together with opportunity for conversation, the stronger our relationship is, and our parenting skills are better too."

Sometimes we need to spend a little more time and money and energy on our marriages.

The above list gives ideas for simple dates. What about ROMANCE?

One friend wrote, "One of the best things my husband and I did was take some time off and go to Hot Springs, Montana. We stayed at a place with private plunges. Plunges are large hot tubs without the jets—like a soaking pool. Our whole purpose was to be together and communicate. It helped restore our love and commitment."

Someone else wrote, "Once a year we like to go to a motel in another city. We eat one meal a day in a restaurant and take the rest of our food with us. We might go window-shopping, shop at thrift stores, or go miniature golfing. Nothing too expensive. This time together doesn't take a lot of planning, is fun, and gives us some quality time together. It doesn't hurt our limited financial budget too much."

My husband came home from a men's meeting and said that our pastor had mentioned that our friend Jan was the most romantic man he knew. I said, "He should teach a class to the rest of the men."

My husband said, "No. The rest of us men should re-educate him."

So I have asked Jan for his suggestions. Single ladies, don't ask for Jan's address, he is married. You are out of luck. Married men, don't complain to me if your wife hands you these suggestions from Jan. You need to deal with him yourself. However, I did promise him I wouldn't give out his address or phone number. Here are Jan's suggestions for adding some romance into your marriage:

- Surprise is the key element.
- Plan ahead.
- Getting away from the house adds romance.

Jan said the most romantic thing he did was about ten years ago. His wife still remembers it and agrees. It was on Valentine's Day. He made reservations at a small restaurant. He had flowers on the table. Inside the card were two tickets to a concert. Afterward, they spent the night in a fancy hotel.

Jan likes to take his wife to bed-and-breakfast places. She really enjoys going too.

This year was our friends' twenty-fifth wedding anniversary. To celebrate they took a cruise. The husband said, "I came home with a renewed appreciation for my wife and also a new perspective on our communication styles that I think has helped me a lot in communicating better. Just spending that much time together, with really no place else to go, and with the resolve not to be working on some project, was very important in strengthening our relationship, not only because of enjoying each other's company but also because of being able to see things that needed improvement."

We might not all be able to go on a cruise, but maybe we can snatch a weekend or a couple of days during the week once or twice a year. Some couples say they do this once a quarter. Maybe when we can't take a week or a day, we can take an hour.

Most of the people who responded to my question about dating felt it was a matter of priorities. Even when our marriages are a priority, we may not have the time or money to do the things we would like to do.

If you don't have any time or any money, what can you do to put romance into your life?

One woman told me, "One night a week our son needs to be picked up at his school at 9:15. My husband and I go early and sit and talk and kiss—it is neat!" I would say there's one couple that has the idea!

Other couples said they left notes:

- In lunch boxes.
- On pillows.
- In briefcases.
- In suitcases or folded up in clothes, when their spouse traveled.
- On their spouse's desk at home or the office.
- On the mirror first thing in the morning or last thing at night.
- On the computer.

Some of these couples also said, "Send notes through e-mail to home or office computer or use the regular mail."

One woman says just a quick phone call from her spouse to her at work saying "I love you!" means a lot to her. Someone else said, "Leave a message on his/her voicemail—but make sure it's his/hers. Remember too, that many companies monitor their employees' messages, so what you say may not stay private."

Another friend told me "One of the most romantic things my husband did was, without my knowing it, he went out and bought the music to our song. When we were alone, he played it on the stereo."

You might like to plan a date away from home. Do something that doesn't take any money or time to prepare; for example, a walk in the park or go stargazing or bird watching. If you live in the city and can't get out in nature, pick up a video from the library of a country or place you'd like to take your mate. If you are single, plan a date with a friend.

If we approach our marriages as a priority in our lives, then maybe we could use some help with ideas. If you can't afford to buy books, how about going to the library? One book I found is *1001 Ways to Be Romantic,* by Gregory J. P. Godek, published in 1995 by Casablanca Press. If you're wondering how making romance a priority simplifies your life, consider this thought from *1001 Ways to Be Romantic:* "5 minutes devoted to romance = 1 day of harmony."

Chapter 18

Travel Light

We were helping relatives with their luggage. A friend standing beside me looked around at the luggage being tugged around the large airport. He said, "Watching all these people fight with their luggage reminds me why I only like to travel once every two or three years!"

I know what he means. Four years ago we were some of the ones lugging luggage. My husband, son, and I spent twenty-one days in Europe. We traveled by car through England, Scotland, France, Germany, Austria, and Switzerland.

Each night we lugged everything into our rooms and each morning lugged it out to the car! Each of us had only one suitcase for clothes and personal items. However, we thought that in some of the areas we might camp. We had a duffel bag filled with sleeping bags and pillows. One suitcase contained three pads for under the sleeping bags, some food, and a small backpacking one-burner camp stove. Another suitcase had a tent, cooking utensils, more food, and six rolls of toilet paper. We spent one night camping!

In Austria we were in the cleanest campground we have ever been in. However, all night trains whizzed by just down the hill from our tent. My husband and son slept. Every time a train went by, I thought we were in the middle of an earthquake.

We came back from our trip with five and a half rolls of toilet paper! The toilet paper in Western Europe is quite adequate. However, I have heard that in certain countries in other parts of the world you need to pack your own.

Next time, we are only going to take one carry-on piece of luggage and buy our food and anything else we might need over there. I don't think we will be camping!

So my first recommendation is: Know your plans!

My friend J. T. gave this advice on being prepared to travel:

- Keep your bags packed.
- Keep your passport current.
- Keep your papers in order.
- Try to avoid checking any luggage on airplanes.
- Try to get an aisle seat as far forward as possible so you can exit rapidly.

Well, J. T., I think I might have cured one man of your theory about sitting in the aisle seat. We were coming home from Florida. There had been a mix-up in our seating arrangements. At the ticket counter we managed to get things straightened out. As we walked out to the boarding area, my husband said, "Row ten. That's right behind first class. We will be one of the last ones to board. All of the storage places will be taken. We will be lucky to get any space in the overhead racks for all this stuff. I told you we should have checked more."

"I certainly wasn't going to check this box of oranges," I said. "And I might need something out of this carry-on and that other bag. Don't be such a worrywart, we won't have any problems. Besides, we are each allowed two pieces of carry-on luggage."

Don was right. We were some of the last to get on the plane. When we did board and get to our assigned seats, there was a gentleman sitting in the aisle seat. He graciously got up and stood further down the aisle. He waited for us to put our luggage away and get seated. However, as much as I hate to admit it, Don had been right, again. All the overhead storage was full. So we held up all the remaining passengers as we tried to find places to stack our luggage. Finally our seatmate moved into one of the other rows of seats. He remained standing. My husband moved farther down the aisle to wait for a stewardess to help. (You could tell he was my husband because he had a red face and kept muttering, "I told you we should have checked this stuff!")

The patient young man waiting behind me asked, "May I help you?"

"No, thank you," I answered, "We might have to rent a trailer and tie it to the tail wing, but we'll get everything in."

A man sitting across the aisle said, "Just a case of taking too much stuff."

I thought his remark deserved a comment, so I answered , "It is not! The man at the store where I bought that carry-on luggage said it would fit in the overhead bin. Besides, it was designed by an airline pilot."

"That doesn't matter," the "nice" man across the aisle replied.

Right about then I realized I should keep quiet or I might be walking from Florida to Washington State.

Finally we managed, with the help of a stewardess, to get things stored.

Don might have been thinking his life would have been simplified if my seat had been out on the wing!

I turned to the man beside me. The one who had been so patient about waiting for us to get seated. "I'm sorry to have kept you standing so long. How did you get on sooner than we did?" I asked.

He answered, "I travel so much I'm allowed to be one of the first to board."

I don't know, but I think I might have cured that gentleman from ever wanting to sit in an aisle seat again. So you see, J. T., maybe your tip should be don't sit in an aisle seat!

Other travelers gave their tips:

- Tie a piece of colored rope, string, or other material around the handle of your luggage. You can spot it more quickly.
- Leave the kids at home!
- If traveling by air, travel at night.
- Plan ahead. Map it out. Know what is ahead.
- If traveling by car, plan on one meal in the car—you can eat it at a rest area and save time and money.
- Always bring wet wipes or a wet washcloth in a plastic bag.
- Travel light. Limit "stuff." Enjoy the trip.
- Travel only by plane for long trips.
- Take less makeup.
- Take a luggage carrier.
- If traveling by car, bus, or train, take a small icebox.
- Have a bag containing your cosmetics ready to go all the time. Place a list in the bag with the rest of what you need to take. No thinking. No forgetting.
- If traveling by car, stop often to stretch your legs.
- Keep your sense of humor.

Jamie put her advice simply: "Pillows, blankets, cooler, picnic basket, and rest stops! You need all of these to simplify traveling by car!"

I wonder. If we were like turtles and had to carry everything on our backs, how much luggage would we take?

A number of people said their biggest concern when traveling is their clothes. What to take, how much to take, and how to care for them. Some seasoned travelers gave the following ways that helped them in making those decisions:

- Take enough clothes for only four or five days and plan to wash them if your vacation is longer.
- Take clothes that are one color, so you can take only one pair of shoes for dress and one for casual.
- Dress comfortably.
- Take clothes that don't need ironing.
- Roll all your clothes. (This was quite a popular answer, but I haven't tried it yet.)
- Take half the clothes you think you will need.
- Take a comfortable pair of shoes.
- Buy an outfit that can be made dressy or casual just by adding a little or taking away a little.

One weary traveler stated, "There are no easy ways to simplify travel other than to stay at home!"

How do you keep track of your spouse, child, or friend who is traveling with you? I forgot to ask my friend Bill's advice. I'm sure he would have had some. He told me this story.

"On one vacation we took the train. On the return trip to Seattle, the conductor made the announcement that the vista dome car would be going to Portland. The rest of the train was going to Seattle. My wife and three children were in the dome and didn't hear the announcement. My mother, one of my children, and I were down in another car. I had all the money. My wife and three children went to Portland. My mother, one child, and I went to Seattle. Two Catholic sisters helped my wife take care of my children. They even read stories to them. The conductor allowed my wife and children to eat in the dining car. So she owed money for all the meals. That was one trip we will never forget!"

Traveling can be what you make it! However, if you learn to travel light, it can add to your comfort.

Chapter 19

Break for a Vacation

"The most important thing to remember about vacations," Marsha said, "is to realize sometimes shorter is better." She continued, "It takes me two days to relax, but two weeks might be too long."

I bet most of us have had vacations when we have needed a second vacation to recover from the first vacation. Some of us may have been told we are on vacation all the time!

Honestly, ladies, here is one from Katie. "Being a homemaker, I'm always on break. Getting my work done is my problem." I just about didn't put her comment in this book and certainly didn't use her real name.

A vacation according to the dictionary is "to be free from a duty or service." Katie might need a break from being a homemaker. The career person might need a break from his/her career. What might be a break for one person might be work for another. We need to pick what is best for us—what would really free us from our regular duties.

Since a vacation is a change of pace, I asked people what things they did for a change of pace, when they couldn't get away from home. Here is what they found relaxing:

- Listening to soft music
- Watching a sunrise or a sunset
- Working on a jigsaw puzzle
- Reading a funny book
- Rocking a child to sleep
- Playing a game on the computer
- Doing something nice for someone else
- Playing with the children
- Playing word games
- Reading or writing letters
- Talking to a friend on the phone
- Working on a craft or hobby
- Singing—Some of us can only sing when no one else is around. We might relax, but everyone else might be uptight from our singing off key. It might be a way to get the house to ourselves.
- Playing a musical instrument
- Soaking in a warm, sudsy bath
- Working in the garden
- Taking a nap in the middle of the day

A minivacation might simplify your life by giving you just the break you need to make it through your week.

Some people can relax better in their own home. But other people can never fully relax in their home because they always see something they "should" be doing. Those people may need to get away for a vacation. For longer breaks, when they had a day or two or three, some people like to:

- Take a trip to the beach
- Take a short trip by plane, train, bus, or ferry

- Take a trip to the mountains and stay at a cabin
- Take walks in the woods
- Visit local areas of interest such as the zoo or planetarium
- Visit relatives
- Attend a program they have always wanted to go to
- Attend a women's retreat
- Take a hike or play physically challenging games like tennis
- Go antiquing to other cities or states

What about longer, more expensive vacations? Here is what a friend wrote after he and his wife had gone on a vacation: "There's a bit of a twinge of guilt at spending so much on a vacation—we'd never done anything expensive or luxurious for vacation. I think it was very justified, and couples ought to plan toward big celebrations on a regular basis. Who knows, we might decide to do something like that every five years from now on. Life is short. We ought to do things we'll look back on with pleasure and joy."

I agree with him. At least once or twice in a lifetime, it might be nice to save up and take the vacation of our dreams. We might have to wait until the children are grown. We can set a goal and work toward it. For example, we planned to spend three weeks in Europe the summer between my son's junior and senior high school years. For a year before we went to Europe, my husband delivered phone books door to door on his days off from his regular job. Occasionally I went with him, but because I can't do very much physically, I just went along for moral support. We might never be able to take another vacation like it, but that European vacation holds memories I will always cherish.

I think what my friend told me, about how they simplified on their cruise, might help anyone to simplify any vacation. Here is what he said. "We found the best values we could on a cruise. We didn't splurge on unnecessary things like drinks brought to you by a waiter while you're sitting by the pool. We didn't waste any money in the onboard casino. We didn't come back with a single piece of tourist kitsch. We've done that on other trips, and the junk just ends up in a box, waiting for the day it looks old enough to be thrown away! We spent everything we could to make sure it was a good cruise. We didn't question spending another two hundred dollars to get the best shore tours we could—going to places we really wanted to go. We managed to get a free upgrade to an outside cabin with portholes. To me the portholes were a very nice feature I wouldn't have wanted to do without."

Do you have a vacation you dream about? What is it? Write it down where you can see it. You can always dream. If you can't go, can you find books, videos, and/or attend travelogues to learn about where you want to go? Maybe you will never get to go, but you will have added a dimension about learning something.

Instead of moaning and feeling unhappy that you can't go, you will have improved your life by doing something about your dreams.

I have always wanted to go to Australia, and I would like to take a second trip to Europe. I hope to go someday. However, even though I've always wanted to go to Brazil, because of my health I probably will never get to go. But I have read about it and talked to people who have lived there. Just this week, my husband and I went to eat in a restaurant. The host was a young student from Brazil. Because I had read a little about it, I could ask him a few questions. His face just lighted up when we showed real interest and knowledge about his country. Our lives were enriched too.

Chapter 20

Take a Hike

"Keep healthy even if all you can do is take a hike. Walk every day. Your life becomes a lot more complicated when you have to deal with an illness," Max said. He knows. He is living with a chronic illness.

Max continued, "Those who are healthy will need ways to simplify staying healthy, and those who have chronic illnesses will need ways to simplify dealing with their illness."

Sometimes just little things will help us meet Max's goals.

Look at the things that people recommend you can do to help yourself stay healthy. Notice that most of the ideas that were given are free to do. The time that you take to do them depends on the amount of time you have or want to take.

- Walk each day. If you can't walk outside, walk in your home. Put on a bouncy tune and march up and down. You may want to walk in a shopping mall. (Just keep your hands in your pockets

so you won't buy anything, or go before the stores open.)
- Take vitamins each day.
- Make sure to do something relaxing, even if you only have fifteen minutes.
- Turn off all outside stimuli such as TV, radio, and phone for a period of time each day.
- Work in the garden each day.
- Walk your dog.
- Have a deep, meaningful conversation with someone you haven't talked with in a while. Ask them about their problems and really listen. You might find out that what is happening in your life isn't all that bad.

Stress can be a big factor in some people's lives. Dennis, a pastor friend, says, "I am constantly dealing with people problems. I found that if I was to stay healthy, I needed to do something to relieve stress. What helped me was to make something with my hands. I now make cedar planters and buckets. I call my cedar buckets 'friendship buckets' and give away a lot more than I have ever sold. This made my life more interesting while reducing the stress."

Learn what helps you to relax and do it.

Whether you are healthy or dealing with a chronic disease, you might feel better by doing what some people with chronic diseases said they do to live healthier lives. Here is their list:

- Do just what you have to.
- Learn to pace yourself.
- Start being content with a simple day.
- Begin to say No to Christian people and Christian things.
- Realize you might have to reduce your "to do" list.

Even little steps help people with chronic illnesses cope. People living with chronic diseases told how they simplify their lives:

- Went to physical therapy and learned how to balance and think about walking when I am walking
- Began taking extra vitamins
- Began using a cane to walk
- Began using an electric scooter to get around. (I've watched the elderly gentleman next door who has so much more freedom to get around and can do so much more than he could before he had his scooter.)
- Took courses on how to deal with my disease
- Learned to ask for help if or when I needed it
- Used the Internet to get information
- Exercised each day—either by walking a little or even when in bed or my wheelchair.
- Began to swallow my pride and use a disabled sticker
- Went to a support group
- Remembered I felt better when I took my medication

Speaking of medication, my friend Manda who has multiple diseases, says she has simplified taking medication. Here is her story in her own words:

"I have to take umpteen pills every day—most of them in the morning or at bedtime. It got to be an ordeal to take each pill out of their separate bottles every time I was to take them. I started using a weekly pill divider. One divider for my morning pills and another one for my bedtime medication. But that meant a huge amount of time every Sunday fixing up the week's supply. I hated doing that. I finally bought two of those fairly large, divided boxes that are made for people who take lots of vitamins. I can pour a three-month supply of medium to small pills into each section so I don't have to do that step over and over every week. When I take my morning and evening pills, I only have to open one thing. I can tell at a glance if something is running low. If I spend the night away from home, I carry my box. I don't have to haul out my list of medications and make sure that I have them all and that I have enough to last.

"I even had a color photocopy made of some pansy fabric I liked and decoupaged it to the outside of the box that has my night pills. I can tell the boxes apart instantly, and so can hubby when he's sent after one.

"I have carefully labeled each divider with the name and strength of each medication so that: (1) I can remember their names and strengths if I see it enough times; (2) I won't miss anything; and (3) if I need to have someone else get out my medications, they'd know what was what.

"When I finally got smart enough to order and fix these up, it really simplified my life."

Whether we are healthy or dealing with a disease, there are little things we can do to help ourselves feel better. When we feel better, our lives will be simplified.

Chapter 21

Enjoy Your Guests

Do your guests feel comfortable? Do you? Three-year-old Timmy and his parents were visiting his grandparents. Timmy had been good all day. However, at the dinner table, he kept squirming and moving and looking under the table. "Timmy, be still!" his mom kept saying. Finally she asked, "Timmy, what is wrong?"

"There's a creature under there," Timmy said as he pointed under the table.

Everyone looked—at a dead rat.

Other than making sure you don't have a dead rat under your table, what can you do to help both you and your guests feel at ease?

Inviting dinner guests

Do you think that using your best china and having an elaborate dinner is the way to make someone feel comfortable? Not according to Erna. Erna had just moved to a different town where she taught school. After church one week a woman came up to her and said,

"I'm a teacher too, and I'm tired too. But I would like you to come to our home for dinner. Will you?"

Erna said, "I went home with that lady and her husband. They had a dining-room table with a beautiful lace tablecloth. However, we sat at the small kitchen table. My hostess served tomato soup and cheese sandwiches. After we finished eating, we went into the living room. They each sat in their favorite chairs, and I sat on the couch. We all felt so comfortable that soon we started to nod and slept for a while. That was many years ago, and that couple are still some of my dearest friends. It didn't bother me that she didn't use her best china and tablecloth. I was relaxed knowing she was just being herself."

Many of the folk that I interviewed about simple ways to have guests said, "Just be yourself."

For example, Rose lives in Africa and often has guests. Many times they are traveling from one part of the country to the other, and sometimes she doesn't have much notice. Most of the time she serves applesauce or fruit salad. She makes a gravy and adds beans. She serves the gravy and beans with cornbread or pancakes for breakfast. For supper she serves them with rice.

Fruit salad or applesauce, a gravy with beans served with cornbread or pancakes or rice. What a simple menu! Many of us might use the same menu, but because we have different personalities we would do it differently. Some of us would rather make the cornbread, while others would choose to buy it. Some would prefer to make the pancakes, while others of us would rather pour rice into a pot to cook.

Quite a few women said they simplified by having a potluck. They asked people to bring a dish or two. One friend says, "The best times are the spur-of-the-moment potlucks when you say, 'Bring what you have. Come over to our house or meet us in the park.' That way no one has to worry about having a fancy dish or spotless house."

So, why not try having a spur-of-the-moment potluck at your home, your church, or a park?

If everyone brings a dish or two, those with food allergies can bring something they can eat.

Just yesterday, I leaned over to a lady sitting beside me in church and said, "We can't have you over this week, but in a couple of weeks we'd like to have you come to share our dinner."

She whispered, "I'd love to, but I'm on a severely restricted diet."

"That's OK," I answered. "Would you be comfortable bringing your own food?"

"Yes," she whispered back. I thought to myself, that is the ultimate in simplifying having guests over to share dinner. Have them bring their own! Now I'm trying to figure out a way to say, "Come for dinner, but please bring your own food!" Then I could add, "Bring enough for us too." I wouldn't have to cook at all. Now that's simple!

Overnight guests

Having overnight guests is a little different than having guests for a meal. Other than saying "Please bring your own sleeping bag," I haven't figured out a way to say "Bring your own bed or at least your own sheets!"

My Florida friends, J.T. and Bonnie Shim, have a bed and breakfast. They also both have jobs away from home. J.T. maintains that having guest guidelines simplifies their lives. We may not have a bed and breakfast, but I think that J.T. has a point. Maybe we could learn some things from them.

"Rules help to set expectations," J.T. says. He adds, "Some of the reasons for using guidelines include: not having to repeat the rules; they can be sent ahead of time so people know what to expect and how to pack; there are standardized rules for everyone so people won't think they are just for them."

Another friend disagrees. She doesn't have rules for her friends. I think it would depend on your personality and the situation, but, like J. T. explains, "If you do have them, you can avoid problems."

J. T. and Bonnie have graciously consented to sharing their guidelines with us. Here is an abbreviated and adapted version of their guidelines. The comments in square brackets are the author's, not J. T.'s or Bonnie's.

Welcome. We are glad you can share some time with us. To make life easier and safer for everyone, allow us to share some ideas, idiosyncrasies, and standard operating procedures with you.

- Unless other arrangements have been made, all guests are expected to have their own transportation. So that we can get in and out of our garage, please park on the road—but not in front of the mailbox. The mailman doesn't want to go through your car to deliver the mail. Also, since Bonnie and J.T. "fight" to see who can get the mail first—we need no more competition.
- For your own safety, please acquaint yourself with the location of smoke detectors, fire extinguishers, phones, phone numbers, and means of rapid evacuation and alternative routes. To preclude the need for such emergency procedures, please do not use alcohol, cigarettes, firearms, explosives, or unattended open flame.
- Please conserve resources. For example, turn off the lights when not in use.
- Always lock all windows and doors. While this is a safe neighborhood, we don't want to encourage trouble.
- Whenever possible, do not permit non-guests onto the property without prior clearance from us.
- In the event of an emergency, call 911. An emergency is defined as danger to yourself or our property.
- In an emergency, please also contact us at work. [Both

J.T. and Bonnie give their work numbers and their cell phone numbers.]

- You are welcome to the food in the refrigerator. [If you are not comfortable with that, specify when guests come, what they can and can't eat.]

- You are welcome to use the washer and dryer when they are not in use. [Some people don't want others to use their washer and dryer. You might say, "Please have me put your clothes in for you" or "Please do not use the washer and dryer."]

- Please rinse all dishes and put in dishwasher.

- If you plan to return to the house late, let us know in advance. This will prevent us from mistaking you for an intruder.

- If we need to modify the temperature for your comfort, please tell us.

- We allow guests to bring well-behaved small pets.

- Please only feed our pets their own pet food and at the times specified.

Thank you for coming. Enjoy your stay.

J. T. and Bonnie also send instructions and a map on how to get to their place. They include a list of events, parks, and other tourist spots.

Other people had ideas too. One lady said, "I don't feel like I need to wait on my guests. I ask them for their help if I want it."

Mary said, "The key to being hospitable is making our guests feel loved."

Could acceptance be the key to hospitality? By accepting ourselves, being ourselves, and accepting others, we would then be free to enjoy our guests.

Chapter 22

Modern Conveniences: Help or Hindrance?

Do modern conveniences simplify or complicate your life? Which ones do you use the most? Which one would simplify your life if you got rid of it?

Modern conveniences include phones, television, computers, microwaves, and other inventions that seem useful to someone. Some people use certain conveniences to simplify life, while other people think if they could get rid of those same conveniences, their lives would be less complicated. I think it depends on the person's situation and how they use that convenience; for example, cell phones.

Elvin said, "I simplified my life this past year by getting rid of excess things and services that weren't enhancing my life. No more beepers. No more cellular phone. No more call waiting. I save about one hundred fifty dollars a month."

However, Valerie said, "My cell phone is one modern convenience I just couldn't be without. It has saved me many hours. My children can contact me at any time. When I have been trying to find someone's house, I have picked up the phone and called. Before I might have had to drive many miles to find a pay phone. I feel a lot safer just having one in my car. I know help is just a phone call away."

I agree with Valerie. I believe, for safety's sake, it is important to have a cell phone in the car. However, talking on a cell phone while driving is dangerous! I think people should pull to the side of the road to use their phones. But having people pulling off and on the side of the road can be hazardous too. It might get so bad we will need "phone" lanes on our highways!

Maybe if we are trying to live a more calm and peaceful life, Carrie had the best answer. She said, "Increased technology bombards us with information. Maybe we need to control what comes into our lives by radio, television, computers, and newspapers. I feel a lot better, a lot calmer, when I have not listened to the news for a whole day."

The television was what most people say they'd like to get rid of to simplify their lives. Some said they, or a family member, had trouble turning it off. However, many people who live alone say just to have the television on, even if they are not looking at it, helps them to feel like someone is in the house with them.

My husband told me he thought he was a modern convenience. He wondered if I would want to simplify my life by getting rid of him. I shot him a quick smile. "No, you're an antique. I'd better keep you!"

What convenience simplified lives the most? Microwave was the answer that over half the people gave. Others said, stove, refrigerator, washer and dryer, vacuum cleaner, or food processor.

Whether a modern convenience simplifies your life or not depends upon how you use it. Some suggestions people gave for using modern conveniences:

- Put small kitchen appliances where you can use them without having to bend down into a cupboard to get them out.
- Get rid of all those appliances you don't use.
- Think before buying any gadget: How am I going to use it? Will it

simplify my life? Will I use it or just store it? How long will it take for me to learn to use it? How long will it last? How much will it cost to maintain it? Do I have to make a choice between it and something else that might mean more to me? Just because someone else has something doesn't mean that it will simplify my life.

- Don't answer the phone—use an answering machine. Only answer the calls you want to.
- Get caller ID to help screen your calls.
- Tell each telemarketer who calls to place your number on their "do not call list."

My son and daughter-in-law, who worked for a short time in telemarketing, said that if you get telemarketing calls, you can ask the telemarketers to take your name off of their list. I just talked with a telephone representative. She gave me the following advice, "Get off telemarketing lists by writing a note to the following address: Telephone Preference Service, Direct Marketing Association, P. O. Box 9014 Farmingdale, NY 11735-9014. List all names and phone numbers that you want deleted from telemarketing." It may take a while before this works, but one friend reports that after about nine months he is no longer getting any telemarketing calls.

Remember that how and why you use your modern conveniences can simplify your life. It will depend on your lifestyle.

Chapter 23

Pardon Your Garden

How can you pardon your garden? By that, I mean how can you have a garden without spending hours working and taking care of it?

I pardon my garden because it is full of weeds! And since my husband's idea of gardening is mowing the grass, I needed some advice for this chapter, so I asked two ladies I know who are master gardeners. Jill and Irene always have beautiful gardens.

Jill gave these hints:

- Plant only low-care perennials or shrubs. Get rid of any plants that are high-maintenance.
- If you like birdbaths, use only those that can be hosed down and filled up again—those that take only a couple of minutes to clean.
- Have sections with paths. Always make each part accessible from a path.

- Make each section small enough so you can take care of it in fifteen minutes. When I was growing up, we had such a large garden it was overwhelming to us children to weed.
- Make paths that aren't high maintenance; for example, beauty bark doesn't have to be watered or cut.
- Have a sink outside so you can wash off your vegetables before bringing them into the house. You can have a compost bin next to your sink so you can just throw the waste parts of the vegetables into it.
- Know your plants. Some perennials multiply like crazy; then you are overwhelmed and have to take them out.
- For people who don't have enough room to have plants, you can get lots of vegetables to grow on stakes in containers; for example, cucumbers, tomatoes, squash, peas, beans.
- Make gardening a pleasure. In the spring. Work in your garden in the early evening when the birds sing. Have a place to sit and read in your garden.

Here is Irene's advice:

- If you like cut flowers, plant just one row or a couple of rows of flowers to cut. Don't spoil the landscape by planting plants you will be cutting flowers from in with the other plants.
- Have a very small garden. Learn how to get a lot of produce off a small area.
- Plant gladiolas close together so you can tie them up or pick them more easily.

One friend says, "I simplify having a garden by buying large plants. I can tell what they are, and it is harder for me to kill them."

Someone else said, "For many years I lived in foreign countries. I wanted a large flower and vegetable garden. I have had a large garden for a few years. Now I am cutting back to easy-care perennials. I am retiring from spending hours in my garden."

Whether a garden would simplify or complicate a person's life depends on the person.

Jill says, "I told my husband I could never live anywhere that I couldn't have a garden. It calms and soothes my soul to work in it."

However, Reanna disagrees. "I don't have a garden and don't feel guilty."

"Gardening helps me to keep healthy," Brenda says.

I'm glad the good Lord made us all different. We can choose for ourselves whether to have a garden or not. If you do have one, don't make it larger than you can easily take care of.

Chapter 24

Retire Happy

"My retirement years are the happiest years of my life," Joan said. "I can do what I want and go where I want. I don't need to make any excuses. People just see this white hair and say, 'Oh, that poor old lady, if she's happy just leave her alone!'"

How can retirement be the happiest years of your life? If you are retired, what can you do to simplify your life? If you are not retired, what are some of the things you can do now to make your life easier when you are retired?

To find some answers, I interviewed the people who should know—retired people.

Callie said, "No one used to talk about retirement. Very few people planned for it. Some people don't leave enough flexibility in their finances or plans. They get locked into situations they can't get out of. For example, friends of mine thought they'd like to move to a certain town. They spent all of their money moving and buying a new place. They found they don't like the new area."

Here are some ideas retired people gave for a happier retirement:

- Start years before retirement to save financially, so you can be financially independent. Plan to live to 100, then you will have enough!
- Have some idea ahead of time where you want to live. Make alternative plans. This frees you to change if you don't like the decision you have made.
- Shop only once a week.
- Get rid of dust collectors. If you have collections you want to keep, put them into glass cupboards.
- Get rid of things that will take extra money and time to maintain.
- Don't buy anything you can't swallow or use up.
- Have a hobby.
- If you like to travel but are by yourself, get someone else to travel with you. Just make sure you are compatible.
- Find something you can do to help others.
- Exercise to keep fit.
- If you are giving things away, have each child write a list of what he/she might want. (Include each child even if they are estranged from the family.) Put all lists together. Everyone then might be able to have at least one choice of what they want. This helps prevent hard feelings because the one who might not ask will still get a choice. (One reader said this really helped her to make decisions.)

One of the biggest decisions people facing retirement have to make is where to live. I asked many people where they lived. Here are some of their comments:

- With my children. I'm not healthy enough to live alone. I help them by baby-sitting my grandchildren.
- One state for the summer, another for the winter
- Near my children
- In the country

- In a retirement community and I love it
- In an apartment in a small town
- In an apartment in the city, where I can attend a lot of activities without needing a car

You can see that people make decisions for their retirement based on their personalities, finances, and health.

Some retired people said the following things would help to make their lives easier:

- Having my children closer
- Having my grandchildren come to stay, but only for two or three days
- Having my children reduce their dependence on me
- Not cutting back on anything I enjoy keeping busy

My friend Susie said, "My mother simplified my life immeasurably by selling her home and moving into an apartment before her death. I'm beginning to think owning a home and property at age eighty is inappropriate. I'm about to suggest that it should be the age of giving away treasured items. My mom had everything legally in order. In several days, my sister and I were able to clean things up. What a gift Mom gave to us children!"

Eloise has an eighty-four-year-old mother living alone. She said, "I worry all the time about my mother. There is no such thing as a person being independent. They always have to have someone doing something for them. If it is not a relative, it is someone else."

Maybe one answer could be what some people are doing in a city near where I live. Single people are moving in with older people. The older person provides the home. The single person does the work to maintain the home. They share living expenses. The single person may take the retired person to the doctor or shopping. This helps the young person save money by having a place to live. The two people have to be very compatible, but it is working for some.

Sometimes when older people resist moving into a retirement home, it is because they don't know what is available.

I can still remember my eighty-three-year-old great-grandmother. She would not consider moving into a retirement home. She had one friend who lived in a retirement home who would take a taxi once a month to go visit my grandmother. Finally one day Grandma's friend said, "Lena, it is your turn to come and visit me."

After visiting her friend, my grandmother called my mother. "Margaret, "she said, "I went to visit Ann today."

"Did you like her home?" my mother asked.

"I loved it!" Grandma answered.

"Did you put your name on the waiting list for a room?" Mom asked.

"I sure did," Grandma answered, "they even have men there!"

Whatever decision you make regarding their retirement, it is easier if you plan ahead.

Chapter 25

Pets—Do They Complicate or Simplify?

"Not having a pet would simplify things, but my animals are comforting emotionally, and they help me relax," Shirley said.

"What's to simplify?" Helen wrote, "You have pets to keep you busy and keep your mind off your troubles."

Pet owners loved to share their tips for how they simplified taking care of their pets. Here are some of the things they suggested would help:

- Provide/install a cat/dog door. Yes, even some cats are trained to go outside instead of using a litter box.
- Put up a fence so the animal doesn't have to be supervised when outside.
- Have self-feed containers for cats.
- Have a water container that only needs to be filled once a week.
- Pour cement where the dog likes to dig out.
- Keep animals outside.

8—S.D.S.

- Have your pets neutered.
- Train animals to stay off furniture. Let them have one blanket they can use.
- Have only short-haired pets.
- Put identification collars on your animals.
- Consider cost in time and money before getting a pet.
- Train your animals so you can control them.

No one said that they had trained their animals to read. Jack's uncle might have wished his cat could read.

"My uncle would sit reading his newspaper. His cat would crawl up on to my uncle's shoulders. He would lick my uncle's bald head. After he was through licking my uncle's head, he would jump through the newspaper." Maybe if the cat had learned to read, it wouldn't have destroyed the newspaper!

Besides training their pets, some pet owners wished that they could have servants to take care of pet hair, keeping litter boxes empty, and baby-sitting their pets.

Having a pet may simplify your life, or it may complicate your life. If you are lonely, you don't necessarily have to have a pet. Find a child to give your love to. It could be a relative, a neighbor's child, a friend's child, a child of a single parent at your church, or you could join one of the many clubs where adults help children.

Chapter 26

Plan Your Funeral

"Oh, how I wish Salina had planned her own funeral," Janelle said. "It would have simplified her children's lives, and it would have been more what she would have wanted."

Janelle continued, "Her children argued about everything. First the dress that one of them chose wasn't the right color. Another wasn't the right style. To please everyone they ended up buying a very expensive dress. The same thing happened when they picked out a coffin. They spent thousands more for the coffin than Salina would have wanted. They argued about the flowers. Finally three different arrangements were bought because they couldn't settle on one.

"Salina worked hard and would have wanted the money spent on her funeral to have gone to her children or to a charity. But her death was unexpected, and she hadn't made any funeral plans. It would have been a lot easier on her family if she had planned her funeral."

Mavis commented about a relative's funeral. She said, "At the time of a death, emotions are so complicated. Some people act out of love, some out of guilt. The process of dying is a part of life that people often ignore until they are forced to face it. People should plan their own funeral regardless of their age or health."

"OK, Mavis, what would you suggest?" I asked. "Some people think that planning their own funeral would complicate their lives. Just one more task to do. Some don't want to think about dying."

"Planning their own funeral could give them a sense of peace. They don't have to make a big production out of it," Mavis said. Here is what she suggested:

- Think about what you would like to have done. Make it simple and easy for your family.
- Write it down. Take only fifteen minutes.
- Tell your family where your list is. Leave it in a place where it can be found easily. Not in a safety deposit box somewhere.
- You may want to verbalize to your family what you want, but that might complicate your life!

Last year, my dad verbalized to us want he wanted when he died. Three weeks before he died from cancer, he was telling everyone what he wanted done. He gave suggestions for what he wanted done at his memorial. He also gave very specific instructions for the food to be served at the dinner afterward. His pastor assured him that the ladies from the church would serve what he wanted, that there would be lots of food, and that his family wouldn't have to worry about it.

This did two things for him—let him still be in charge until the end and helped him know that his wishes would be carried out.

As his family it helped us to know what he wanted done. It freed us of guilt. (However, if he had left complicated instructions, some of which we may not have been able to carry out, then we might have felt guilty. He knew what he told us was simple and easy to do.)

Love yourself and your family enough to take the time to plan your funeral.

Chapter 27

Make a Will

"One of the things people put off doing because they think it is going to be too complicated is making a will," Amanda said. "They don't realize that making a will can simplify their lives and the lives of those they love."

Almost everyone who talked to me about wills said they knew a heartbreaking story of family members not speaking to each other because of something that happened with someone's assets. Many had stories of a stepparent and his/her family getting all the assets while the natural children got nothing. Sometimes that would be the parent's choice, but most of the time, because of not making a new will, the person has really decided that his/her children get nothing.

My brother-in-law, Art, who is an attorney agrees. He says, "The biggest mistake people make about wills is not making one. By not making a will, you actually have made one, you just don't know what it is." He thought people might feel like they are hastening their deaths by preparing a will.

Art continues, "Not making a will can set up some bad situations. In our state, if parents die and there is no will or estate plan, each child gets his share when he reaches eighteen. I haven't met an eighteen-year-old yet who can handle that responsibility. The money would be gone very quickly and very unwisely."

Have you made a will? Does it need updating?

Before you prepare a will or have one prepared, Art suggests you think about the following things:

- What are your priorities? What do you want to accomplish with your will? For example, do you have children who would need to be taken care of?
- Write down or outline what your assets are: retirement plans, insurance policies, investments, personal property—house, cars, boats, expensive jewelry, recreation vehicles.

"With most people, the care and education of their children is paramount," Art says. He gives the following tips concerning children and wills:

- People need to choose a guardian for their children. They also need to name a backup person, in case circumstances change.
- A lot of people would have significant money from Social Security that would go to whomever was caring for the children. The children's caretaker would have to show the money was going to the children's benefit.
- If people don't want their children to get all the money at age eighteen, then they need to think of the child's needs and education. Some people have their child get one-half of the money at twenty-five and the other half at thirty. Some like the child to get the first half when he or she graduates with a bachelor's degree from a college. This encourages the child to

get an education.
- One thing most people do not think about is to name one person as a guardian and another person to take care of the trust for the children. (It takes heat off the guardian if the children want money from the trust. Children can make life miserable for their guardian if they figure he/she has control of the purse strings. It is also an extra precaution that the money will be spent like you want.)

In addition to your children, Art recommends you consider:

- What if all the family dies together, where would you want money and things to go?
- If you would like some of your things to go to certain people or have specific instructions, you need to write them down.
- When you want to get a will written, choose an attorney. Some people are queasy and suspicious of lawyers. Shop around for an attorney the same way you might shop for a television or a couch.
- Call around to see what the cost would be for making a will.
- There are computer programs that can be used to write a will. (Art doesn't advise this because they can be incomplete or not state specifics, but he says they might work just fine for some people.)

I wanted to know about the terms *living will* and *living trust*, so Art gave me some definitions.

Living will: A document directing heroic measures not to be carried out if there is no chance of recovery. It states that life supports are to be stopped. In our state, in the state directive to the attorneys, they are to ask their clients about food and water. Does the person wish the living will to state that food and water is to be withheld?

Living trust: Estate planning to avoid probate. All assets are placed in a legal entity. When the person dies, his or her estate does not have to pay money to have the will probated. Probate is the process of transferring the property of the deceased to the heirs and disposing of the debts. In states where lawyers get a percentage of the estate regardless of the time they spend on helping to probate the will, people might save money by having a living trust. However, more and more states are making it easier and cheaper to probate wills. The state will set a reasonable sum, which means the attorney will get paid for the time spent. Also in a living trust you must make sure all your assets are listed. If not, when you die your estate will have to pay for probate. You pay for a living trust when it is written. Out of your funds now. The cost of probate comes out of your estate after you die. Some attorneys have made themselves rich by going around scaring people and having the people set up living trusts. These lawyers usually charge several hundred dollars.

Art says he tends to favor probate. He would in reality usually make more money setting up living trusts. But he feels most people should have use of their money while they are alive, instead of spending it on a living trust. However, it depends on the circumstance.

Other people have shared the following ideas:

- Some organizations will set up a living trust or help make wills at no charge, if your will gives that organization a certain percentage of your estate.
- Keep your will up-to-date. If there are any major changes like remarriage, make sure they are addressed in your will.

I think one of the reasons some of us put off making a will, or put off updating it, is because we are waiting for a large block of time to work on it. It is something we keep putting off until we have the time and it is not a priority. Or it might be we think it is going to cost too much and we don't have the money.

Maybe by breaking the process of preparing a will into easy steps we would actually get one made. The following ideas might help:

- Make preparing a will a priority.
- Write down ideas in a notebook or use your computer to get organized.
- Take fifteen minutes a day for a week or two to collect ideas and financial information.
- Shop for an attorney or another aid to make a will.

Making out a will can simplify our lives by giving us the peace and comfort knowing we have done what we could to take care of our children and possessions.

Chapter 28

Simplifying Shopping

Are you a shopoholic? Do you want to simplify your shopping? The first step might be to know the car you are driving. At least that is what my friend Lorretta might have said. She told me her story, and I promised not to use her real name.

"My husband and I were young and living on a college campus. We didn't have a car, so a friend would graciously lend us his car when we had to drive into town. One day, I had to go to a town about fifteen miles away. Our friend gave me the keys. I noticed as I got into the car that there was a cushion on one seat and some clothes that had been dry cleaned were hanging up in the back seat. I drove into town and parked the car, and when I finished my shopping, I came back to the car. As I opened the door, I noticed that the cushion and the clothes were missing. *That's strange*, I thought, *I wonder what could have happened to those things?* I drove back to the campus, and I saw our friend and gave him his keys. 'I'm sorry,' I said, 'I don't know what happened to your cushion and clothes.'

"Right away, he guessed what had happened. We got my husband and hurried back to town to the police station. The police officer was on the phone and as we stood there waiting for him to help us, I could hear him say, 'What make and color did you say it was?'

"I knew he must have been talking about the car I had driven home. 'Just a minute, I have that car,' I said.

"The police officer put down the phone. He checked and sure enough. I had taken the wrong car! It was the same make, same model, same color—and the key fit! The cars had been parked only a few spaces apart. Somehow the campus photographer heard about what happened, and as we walked into the police station, he walked in behind us. Not only do I have a picture to prove I took the wrong car, but so does everyone who has a yearbook for that year!"

Some women told me it is safer if they don't go shopping. Safer for them, safer for their pocketbook, and safer for their marriage.

However, there are times when we all need to shop. The tips I received on how to simplify shopping were in two main groups: grocery shopping and all other shopping. For the hints for grocery shopping, see chapter 10, "Spare the Cook." The hints on all other shopping can be categorized into three parts: when to shop, where to shop, and how to shop.

When to shop

Some people remarked that a good shopper knows when to shop. Here are their tips on helping you to simplify your life by knowing when to shop:

- Shop once a year for some things such as socks and underwear.
- Shop during the best sales of the year. Make a list and put it on your refrigerator; then you will be ready to shop at the sales.
- Don't buy on the spur of the moment. Go home and think about it. (Or, if you don't like this tip, try the next one!)
- If you see something you really need and like, buy it when you

see it. When you go back to get it, it could be sold.
- Shop early—as soon as stores open.
- Only go shopping when you need to.

Where to shop

Your life can be simplified if you know where to shop, because you can save yourself both time and money. Here are some specific ideas of where to shop, given by thrifty shoppers, to help you be thrifty too:

- Shop at thrift stores.
- Shop at garage sales.
- Buy from catalogues. Faster, cheaper, saves energy.
- Don't buy from catalogues—usually cost more unless they're sale catalogues. Don't forget that you have to pay shipping charges. (These last two ideas are interesting because they probably show different personalities, different financial levels, and different amounts of time people have to shop.)
- Mail bills. This saves time and energy and maybe money. If you go to a department store to pay a bill, you might buy something.

How to shop

Some people felt that knowing how to shop could save you as much time, money, and energy as knowing when and where to shop. Here are their suggestions for how to shop:

- Organize a list of birthdays and special occasions and keep it with you. Buy cards or gifts when out shopping for other things.
- Have a friend shop with you. One who will encourage you to make good choices.
- Make a list of your errands. List them so you have all your errands on the same side of the street.
- Do quite a few errands at the same time or all on one day.
- Don't feel guilty if you can't do all your errands at the same time.

- Leave your credit cards at home. Some people freeze theirs in a block of ice so they have time to think before they use them.
- Learn to recycle things at home.

Whichever ways you choose to shop, do it the way that will simplify your life the most.

Chapter 29

Toss Your Purse

"If you can't find something, ask Jonelle, she's probably hiding it in her purse," Jonelle's husband joked.

It is no joke that you can sometimes find as many things in a woman's purse as you'd find in the corner store. Have you ever picked up a purse—maybe even your own—and asked yourself, "What's in here? It's as heavy as a wheelbarrow full of bricks!"

Have you played a game at a bridal shower, where you get more points for each additional thing you have in your purse? I'm beginning to think that there should be another game started. Instead of winning if you have the most articles in your purse, you should win if you have the least.

As she searched for something in her purse, Marsha sighed, "Are you going to mention simplifying purses in your book?"

My sister said she just took all the receipts and papers out of her purse, and her purse is half the size it was.

"My mother-in-law always used to carry around a large purse.

She ended up needing physical therapy for her shoulder," Molly said. "All I carry around now is a wallet on a strap."

Mavis said, "I have simplified carrying around a purse. I just carry my credit cards, some cash, and my keys. Men just carry their keys and their wallets. Why can't women do the same? Why do we feel like we have to carry everything everywhere we go? We can keep our makeup, hairbrush, address book, or anything else we might need in another bag in the car. When you think about it, it is silly to carry our makeup and everything else into the grocery store or anywhere else."

"But Mavis," I said, "A large purse can be a good thing to use to hit someone with, if they are bothering you."

"Actually, you can move a smaller purse quicker—and with a better aim!" Mavis replied.

Most purses should be classified as lethal weapons. It wouldn't be a concealed weapon, though. But classes on how to use them safely might be helpful. Maybe if we had to get a license to carry one around, we'd be more circumspect in what we packed into them.

Have you ever observed women and their purses as they walk down the aisle in a store or in the common area of a shopping mall? Some women will be grasping their purse tight against their body. They look as though they could grab it and smack you with it, if you come too close. Other women will have their purses swinging from their shoulders. They aren't paying any attention to where it goes or what it does. You're afraid to bend over in the store to pick something up. You might get walloped on the backside. My friend said that when her son was small, he was always getting hit in the head by some lady's purse.

While I waited to talk with the chief of security at our local mall, I thought it might be fun to observe the first 100 women who walked by. What were they doing with their purses? Here is what I found. Forty-eight women weren't paying any attention to the purses swinging from their shoulders. Nineteen women were clutching either the strap or the purse as it dangled from their shoulder. Eighteen women were carrying their purses in their hand. Ten women didn't look like they were carrying purses. Four women had their purses around their neck and over their shoulder. One woman had a fanny pack.

When I finally managed to talk to the chief of security, he told me that purses were becoming a good target for thieves. I asked him, "What are some of the things women should know or should be reminded of that would help them"? Here are the points he made:

- Don't leave your purse in the restroom.
- Don't leave your purse at a telephone booth.
- Don't leave your purse in the changing room while you are out looking in mirrors at the clothes you are trying on.
- Don't leave your purse on the roof of your car while you place your children or packages into your car.
- Pay attention. One person had someone come up to her and distract her as she was walking to her car while another stole her purse.
- Don't put your purse in a shopping cart then leave it or turn around. This often happens in grocery stores.
- Don't lay your purse down so you can examine something in a store.
- Don't make a show of placing a purse or other things in the trunk of the car and then going into a store. If someone is observing, they will think there is something valuable in the trunk.

Based on the above information and observations, there are two things we women need to do to simplify taking care of our purses. The first is to be observant when carrying a purse, and the second is to cut down on what we haul in our purses. Some of the women who are carrying less "stuff" in their purses gave these suggestions:

- Obtain a canvas or other large bag that wouldn't be damaged if something spilled on it. Fill it with your makeup, hairbrush and/ or a comb, an address book, and anything else you might think you would need. Each of these could be put into a different colored zippered or Velcro bag so you could grab them quickly if you needed to. Leave the larger bag in your car. (I haven't tried this yet, but several women suggested it.)
- Use a fanny pack.
- Use a money belt to carry credit cards. Not only is it safer, but credit cards are harder to get to, and you might not spend as much!
- If you must carry a purse, carry a small one.

The one time we might need large purses and to have them full is when we travel. However, once we get to our destination, it is safer to use a smaller purse or no purse at all.

Let's decide on how we can simplify our lives by simplifying what we carry around in our purses.

Chapter 30

Giving Gifts

"The easiest way to simplify gift giving is to recycle a gift someone has given you," Mildred said. "A couple weeks ago, a friend told me she belonged to a women's group that had secret sisters. She had given her secret sister a gift. The very next week, she received the gift back from the woman who had her name." Mildred added, "I laughed and laughed. I didn't say anything. I knew that in a month, when secret sisters were revealed, my one friend would find out that giving someone a gift that you have received from another person can be dangerous!"

"Is gift giving a pleasure or a pain for you?" I asked people. Their answers ranged from "I don't have money to give gifts, so I don't give any" to "I spend hours trying to get just the right gift."

However, a lot of people have ways they simplify their gift giving. Here are their recommendations for your to simplify yours:

- Make handmade things well ahead of time.
- Make homemade gifts, but only ones you enjoy making.

- Use a pretty gift bag and tissue paper. It is faster than wrapping.
- Buy gift bags, wrapping paper, tissue paper, and ribbons on sale.
- Give gift certificates.
- Keep a list of peoples' hobbies and interests with you, so if you find a sale, you will know what to get.
- Give money.
- Give magazine subscriptions.
- Give gifts of fun things to do. Take the person with you to a concert, sports event, or other occasion.
- Give useful gifts like favorite soaps, foods, perfumes, hand lotions—but make sure it is what people will use. My son started me collecting different small versions of the Bible with dusty rose leather covers. This year for my birthday, my husband couldn't find a small Message Bible with a rose cover so he bought one in a different color and had a book binder re-cover it for me. I cherish those gifts.
- Give gift certificates to simplify someone else's life; for example, maid service, garden help, dining out.
- Set a budget for gift giving. Don't use credit cards.
- Buy your own gifts for children or husband to give to you. My sister, who likes a certain calendar, buys her own when she sees it on sale or has her husband do it if he is with her. This year, about a week before Christmas, my eleven-year-old nephew asked his dad, "Have you or Mom bought her calendar yet?" My brother-in-law said "Yes." But I guess my nephew wanted to make sure, so he asked his mom. "Did you get your calendar yet?"
- If money is in short supply, give gift certificates of time or services; for example, washing someone's floor, taking an elderly person to the grocery store, one hour of working in a garden. To a spouse give certificates for back rubs or massages.

Maybe for times when gift giving can become a pain, we need to stop giving. My friend Teri said, "Last year we had spent all year sorting, giving away, and donating stuff we didn't need. In

September we decided we didn't need or want any more stuff."

She continued, "We decided the first step was to notify most of our friends that we didn't want to exchange Christmas gifts. I was careful how I worded the message because I didn't want to offend anyone. We just said, 'God has blessed us and our home, and we have everything we need, so we are bowing out of the Christmas buying. We will still exchange phone calls or letters. We just won't be sending out any gifts.' "

Teri said, "The nice thing was everyone called or wrote back and said they were relieved. They had all been wanting to do the same thing but had been hesitant to do so. It freed up time for us to enjoy the programs, lights, and other festivities of the season. We spent time doing things as a family. We didn't spend our time or money buying things people might not use anyway."

For those you want to continue giving gifts to, consider these tips:

- Plan a trip somewhere; for example, the mountains or the beach, as a family instead of giving gifts—this can become a family tradition. The trip doesn't have to be right at Christmastime.
- Exchange names—draw names from a hat or a bowl and only buy one large gift. Have each person write down a list of what they would like.
- Give gifts at Thanksgiving instead of Christmas. Something that is bought at Thrift stores or yard sales—specify a limit on the money that can be spent.
- Don't over-give—in time, energy, or money.
- Recycle gifts you get but don't use.

One gift I doubt would be recycled is one a friend says she gives. Nan says she knits dishcloths all year and gives them to friends any time during the year. I am sure most people would find Nan's dishcloths so useful they use them in their own kitchens. Receiving them at any time of the year would be a delight.

Sometimes giving surprise gifts during the year is fun to do. Keep them within your time and financial budget. Just one flower or a loaf of homemade bread can say I care. One recent gift that I have received from a friend was some jars of pickles she had made herself. She knows I really enjoy pickles but don't make them. Every time I open a jar or eat one of those pickles I think of her and her generosity.

Other gifts can be given during the year. In my book *Hospitality on a Wing and a Prayer,* I mentioned that I like to give survival baskets to my friends. These are given to people who have lost a loved one to death or divorce, lost a job, been diagnosed with a chronic illness, or are just having a bad week.

One lady told me she adapted the idea and gave a survival box with smaller packages wrapped up with the dates and time to open on them. That way the recipient had something to unwrap over a four-week period. What a nice idea.

Suggestions for simplifying giving gift baskets or packages:

- Buy supplies in bulk—purse-size Kleenex packages, journals, herbal teas.
- Use decorated paper bags, gift bags, gallon jars, or whatever you have on hand as a container.
- Set a budget.
- Don't keep supplies on hand you might eat! I have had chocolate attacks, sugar attacks, or just plain hunger attacks and eaten up my supply of goodies for baskets. I found it was cheaper and healthier if I just bought what I needed for a basket when I did my grocery shopping at the time I was making the basket.
- Instead of putting in a whole box or bag of candy, buy just a few individually wrapped candies you can buy in the bulk section. This is cheaper.

Consider your personality, health, finances, and time when giving gifts. Then gift giving will be a pleasure for you instead of a pain.

Chapter 31

Stay in Touch

Do you like to get cards or notes in the mail? Do you send them? How do you stay in touch with your friends?

Here are ways some folk say they keep in touch with their friends:

- Send little clippings from magazines or newspapers with a short note. I have one friend who, because of illnesses, doesn't get out of her house to shop. However, she always sends me little clippings with a note saying, "I thought you might enjoy this."
- Call them on the phone. Use a timer so you won't go over a specified time limit. Let them know you only have a specified amount of time to talk.
- Keep in touch through your computer (e-mail).
- Buy cards when in the store doing regular shopping so you don't have to make a special trip.
- Organize cards. Instead of just throwing cards into a box or drawer, use a container with dividers. The dividers can be made

from cardboard. Label the divider to organize, for example, birthday, anniversary, get well. A friend does this and says it only took a minute to make dividers, and it saves her time when she is looking to see if she has a card for a certain occasion.

- Make your own return labels or buy them so you don't have to write your return address by hand.
- Send postcards—they're cheaper to send and don't take as long to write. The recipient will know you care. Postcards can be bought in bulk. Ones from the post office are plain but cheaper.
- Send letters, cartoons, or drawings by fax if you have access to one.
- Buy cards whenever you find them on sale throughout the year. You will have them on hand when you need them.

Some people make their own greeting cards. Here are some tips:

- Make your own greeting cards on the computer.
- Make your own cards using rubber stamps.
- Make your own cards using cutouts from magazines.
- Draw your own cards.
- Use your hobby to make cards.

My recommendation is to make your own cards only if you are creative and enjoy it! Otherwise it will put stress into your life instead of simplifying it. I know! I tried making cards with the computer. A friend who makes lovely cards on her computer came to help me. She just kept saying, "That has never happened to me. I haven't seen the computer do that before!" After a couple of hours, I decided it might be a lot healthier for me, and those around me, for me to buy cards!

Christmas is the time of year when a lot of greeting cards are sent. The people I interviewed gave some ideas for specific instructions for sending Christmas cards:

- Send letters instead of cards. Write them on a computer or have

them copied on a copy machine. Add personal notes to each one.
* Start early.
* Don't tell just the good things that happen to you. If you tell how you have handled a problem, it might inspire someone else.
* Buy cards on sale after Christmas for next year.
* Call friends who have local phone numbers.

Send your letters at another time of year when you are not as busy. People will appreciate them more. At least that is what I like to think. It was out of desperation I thought of that one! One year I sent ours out in February. Everyone was shocked and pleased because I'd missed the four years before. Just think, no matter when you send it out, you can give your letter a name:

* In January—a winter letter.
* In February—a love letter or Valentine's letter.
* In March—a spring letter.
* In April—your Easter letter or April fool's letter.
* In May—a May Day letter—if it came from me it probably would be a Mayday letter, written as I was going down for the third time under a load of correspondence.
* In June—a summer letter.
* In July—an Independence Day letter.
* In August—a holiday letter.
* In September—a back-to-school letter—it doesn't matter if you haven't been to school in sixty years!
* In October—a fall letter.
* In November—a Thanksgiving letter.
* In December—whoops! We're back to a Christmas letter.

If you have friends you want to keep in touch with, make it fun and simple. You will do it. If it is time-consuming or expensive, you probably won't do it.

Chapter 32

Holidays, Happy Days?

Are holidays happy days or horror days for you? Some people love any holiday and use it as an excuse to celebrate while other people have chosen to ignore some holidays.

You may choose to ignore a holiday to simplify your life. Good. You have made a decision for you. However, if you ignore a holiday because it brings up sad memories and makes you depressed, you may want to rethink what you can do to make your life happier. You may even start a tradition like Bobbie did.

Bobbie said, "One Thanksgiving my husband and I were going to be alone. I realized we probably weren't going to be the only ones. I made a flyer for our church bulletin for a 'Planned Menu Potluck' at the church. My husband made an announcement in church, inviting anyone who wanted to, to come join us. I made a menu. When people called to say they would come, I asked what they wanted to bring. A week before Thanksgiving, I called everyone and told them what size of dish to prepare. I decorated the room.

This year will be our third year. We have between thirty and forty-five people."

For the person alone with nothing do, planning a dinner like that could put meaning into a holiday. Someone else who is already stressed out doing many different things might want to do what Donna does.

Donna wrote, "All year long we collect aluminum cans and newspapers and take them to a recycling place. We save our money. As a family, we choose either Thanksgiving or Christmas to go out to eat. Everyone likes to see our fund grow during the year. When we go out to eat, we are relaxed and happy."

You may want to do something similar to what Bobbie or Donna do. However, you will want to adapt it to your own situation. Like Bobbie, you may decide to have a potluck dinner with other people. However, you may not want to do the planning. So you might get someone who needs to be busy to do the planning. Or make it truly potluck and don't worry if folk bring similar dishes; for example, salads. Or maybe like Donna, you want to eat at a restaurant, but unlike Donna, you might not want to collect aluminum cans or newspapers.

Do what you need to do to simplify the holiday for you. Most people said it is easier if you plan for the holiday and gave these points for planning to celebrate one:

- Have a budget.
- Have a list.
- Start early.
- Do a little each week.
- Only do what you really, really enjoy and skip the rest.
- Prepare and plan only meals that can be made ahead of time.

Meals can be a big production or be simplified. Here are ways some people simplified making holiday meals:

- Bake and freeze any special goodies ahead of time.

- Make any dinner potluck—Saves the host/hostess' nerves, and everyone is easier to be around!
- Make the food a tradition so you won't have to think about what you are going to cook.
- Be flexible. If you can't make one dish, make another.

To some people, decorating for a holiday is more difficult than preparing the food. From those who enjoy decorating, here are some hints to help you decorate for a holiday:

- Keep decorations simple.
- Put decorations up far enough ahead so you can enjoy them. Do this when you have time. For example, if the holiday is Christmas, you can decorate before Thanksgiving or in October. (I hadn't thought of that one.) Don't worry what others might think.
- Store decorations in order of use. This allows you to put decorations for one holiday away and get out the decorations for the next holiday at the same time. For example, put your Thanksgiving decorations away at the same time you are getting out your Christmas decorations.
- At Christmas use a fake tree. It is easier to take care of, and you can keep it up longer.
- Store tree assembled and with all the lights and decorations on it. Put plastic wrap on it so it won't get dusty. (Some people have family traditions of decorating the tree, this won't work for them.) Storing a decorated Christmas tree! Now that would make decorating for Christmas easier.

There are more tips from others on how to make your holidays easier:

- Use dishwasher-proof plates and silverware or paper plates and paper napkins and plastic silverware.

- Use special dishes for the dinner but have other people help with the cleaning up.
- Draw names for the jobs that need to be done; for example, clearing the dishes off the table, putting the food away, washing the dishes, and drying the dishes.
- Try to use everyone's talents. Those who like to decorate, let them do the decorating. Those who like to cook, let them cook.

Sometimes we can forget in all our preparations for a holiday that our family or friends are more important than the decorations or food. Some ideas that were mentioned for dealing with family and friends during holidays that might help you simplify a holiday:

- Spend time and energy on sharing with others, not on fancy decorations or preparing the food.
- If it becomes a hassle which family to spend Christmas with— husband's or wife's—stay home and start your own Christmas traditions.
- If his family opened their gifts on Christmas Eve and yours opened theirs on Christmas morning—open some at both times or choose a different day entirely. One family likes to keep most of theirs to open for New Year's. Another family likes to give gifts to their immediate family all during the month of December.
- Ask others to share your holiday with you.
- If a holiday really depresses you, plan to take a trip away from home.

One year when there was conflict in their extended family, Cassie and her husband did take a trip. They decided they weren't going to make themselves miserable trying to get along with everyone. Cassie said, "We decided we would go away. We chose a ritzy hotel and had a wonderful time. We even learned a new game. Now our extended family has learned and enjoys that game."

Cassie gives this advice: "If you are depressed about Christmas or around Christmastime, try something different. Don't try to recapture Christmases past. Don't try to do all the family traditions. Another year you may be able recapture the past, or you may start a tradition of your own."

Maybe some of these ideas will work for you. Don't let what others do—such as a sister-in-law or friend—determine what you do. Use your talents, time, energy, and financial situation to make your holiday plans. Don't stress out trying to celebrate any holiday. Simplify in whatever way you want or need to.

Since some people celebrate every little holiday and others ignore all holidays, it doesn't matter what you choose to do.

Happy Holidays!

Chapter 33

Reunions:
Pain or Pleasure?

Sherry says, "I don't go to any of my school reunions. I simplify my life by staying away. I don't like the way I look. My school years were very unhappy years; why would I want to go back to a place where I was so unhappy?"

If that is what works for Sherry, great. However, sometimes by confronting some of the things in life that upset us, we can be more at peace. Then we really will have simplified life.

Family reunions can also be a source of stress. A friend told me a horror story where her brothers and dad fought. Half the family ended up not speaking to the other half.

Since dealing with reunions was what some people felt like they would like to simplify in their life, I asked those who love to go to reunions what they did to help make their reunions happy ones. Most of them stated there was no guarantee a reunion would be happy. But they give ideas on how to simplify going to a reunion and giving yourself a better chance that you would have a good time. Here are their ideas:

- Decide whether going would add stress to your life or simplify it.
- Plan way ahead.
- Try to have some support at the reunion. Encourage someone to be there so you won't feel alone—a spouse, close family member, friend, or classmate.
- Be friendly. Even if you were reserved in school and are still reserved, make an extra effort to say Hello.
- If you are still shy or reserved, write out questions you can ask people or reminders of something funny that might have happened that you can talk about.
- Be yourself—don't try to dress or act like someone else. Don't think you have to rush out and buy new clothes. Whoops—cancel that, ladies! Use it as an excuse to buy new clothes!

Betty said, "Relationships are different than they were in school days. We are adults now and weren't then. We act, interact, and react more maturely now."

This year was our class reunion. It didn't matter that some of us had colored hair, gray hair, white hair, or no hair. It didn't matter that some of us had gained pounds and curves or that some had lost pounds and curves. It didn't matter that some were wealthier than the rest of us. We all accepted each other.

One classmate that I saw about two months after our reunion said she had not gone because she felt like she wouldn't have been accepted. How sad. The key to any reunion is acceptance. If we accept others, they are usually more willing to accept us. If they don't, that is their problem.

The key to helping people feel acceptance is to have someone get personally in touch with them. Some suggestions for making sure everyone is personally contacted:

- Get a lot of people to help. Give each person just a few people to contact or one small job to do.

- Send out notices early. (In some cases, this might mean a year or two before the reunion.) Sometimes we are blessed by surprise reunions. This year that happened to me.

The Detroit airport was crowded. My husband, Don, and I were waiting to board a plane home to Seattle. A couple came to the area where Don and I sat. First, the man sat beside Don. He got up, then his wife sat down. Don leaned over to me and whispered, "Didn't that couple just get off the same plane we did?"

"No," I said. But they did look familiar to me. Especially the woman. Had she given or attended a seminar I had been to?

The wife got up and left. Her husband sat down beside Don again. This time Don asked him, "Did you get off the plane from Philadelphia?"

"No," he answered. "No, we came from Cincinnati. We live in Dayton."

In a few minutes there was an empty chair beside me. When the woman came back, she sat beside me.

"What do you do in Dayton," I asked her.

"My husband is a physician," she said.

" I went to college in Kettering," I stated.

She looked down at the boarding pass in my hand.

"Bev, I'm Vangy," she said.

We gave each other a hug. Vangy had been a high school classmate of mine. I hadn't seen her in thirty-five years. We had been corresponding through e-mail about our thirty-fifth class reunion that was coming up. Don had told me that when he had attended a college back east, he and Vangy had dated a couple of times.

Two months later when I went to our reunion, I at least knew Vangy! With some of the others, although their faces looked familiar, I couldn't put a name with the face. It gave me a smile to see other people lean over and whisper to the person beside them, "That person looks familiar. Do you know who she is?"

This can happen at family reunions too. Especially if it is an emotional time like a funeral. This happened to me last year at my dad's memorial. A woman came through the line where our family was greeting people. I looked at her, and she smiled at me. I said, "I know your face, but I don't remember your name." I saw several smiles and heard many chuckles on down the line.

Then with amazement and laughter in her voice she answered, "Bev, I'm your cousin Shirley."

The woman right behind her, not wanting to take any chances, didn't give me time to embarrass myself again. She said, "I'm your cousin Penny."

Now sometimes when I can't remember something, I'll think back to "I'm your cousin Shirley" and laugh. I'm trying when it comes to names and faces to think of things to say until a person either says her name or I remember it.

At your fifth, tenth, or even twentieth reunion, you might not need help in remembering your classmates' names and faces. But I can guarantee at your thirty-fifth you probably will! Here are some suggestions for reunions for helping to remember what name matches what face:

- Provide blank name tags for people to write their names on and wear. Have people who are not classmates (maybe spouses or friends from other classes) wear name tags too.
- Have women write in maiden as well as married names.

By attending a reunion, you might find out that your life has been enriched by seeing friends again. You might find out that you have dealt with an issue that has bothered you for years and now you are free.

Chapter 34

Belonging to a Church or Other Organization

Being a member of a church or any other organization can be the biggest blessing in our lives, or the biggest curse. If we take on so many jobs that our personal or family life suffers, it can be a real hazard. If, on the other hand, we take an active part, maybe we will get a bigger blessing from whatever organization we have joined. How can we simplify belonging to a church or organization?

The need to simplify becomes apparent when you see a person take on several jobs in an organization and get burned out and then not be able to do anything for several years.

My friend Gina says, "If everyone always says No to everything, churches and organizations couldn't operate. We have to be able to find a happy medium between helping the organization and taking care of ourselves."

Here are hints from people who have found that happy medium:

- Take only one job.

- Take only a part of a big job. You might not be able to be the committee chairperson, but maybe you can do the advertising for the committee.
- Pick the job that will work best for you at this time. If, for example, you have small children, you may want to work in the children's division of a church. If you are single, maybe you would like to work with the single's ministry in your church.
- Rotate years when it is best for you to work. You might not be able to do anything this year, but there's always next year.
- Help with only one project. You might not be able to work in the children's division all year, but you might be able to help with the Christmas pageant.
- Don't spread yourself too thin. Pick only one or two organizations to belong to.

Sometimes there are problems within the organization. Eunice has belonged to many organizations, and she has been the chairperson of many committees. Here are her observations and suggestions:

- Sometimes organizations are clumsily run. They almost collapse. They need to update old ideas. One group was like that. The members needed to get fifteen hours in to get a certificate. The old way was to meet in a group for one hour for fifteen weeks. The new way is to meet as a group for one whole day and two short evenings. More people have joined that group and got their certificate. It is a growing group now.
- People are asked to do many different jobs. They need to make sure they are absolutely good at the job they are asked to do. (Other people say that they don't know if they will be good at something unless they try.)
- People quite often make jobs too detailed. (Here again some people think some jobs aren't detailed enough.)

- One of the biggest hang-ups on a committee is after everything has been explained and thoroughly gone over, there seems as if there is always one person who wants to discuss and discuss . . . and discuss. If it makes a difference in energy, time, or money spent, I don't mind. However, I have sat on committees where one person will hold the whole committee hostage.
- In every organization, in every church, in every city, you have elected leaders and natural leaders. The natural leaders sway public opinion. These natural leaders are especially powerful in small organizations or communities. When organizations realize this, they can make these natural leaders work to their advantage.

In one organization Mabel was made cochairperson with a natural leader. This leader had a lot of good ideas; however, she wasn't willing to let Mabel cochair when she needed to. Mabel resigned about one-third of the way through the year.

We have to know when we can do something and when we can't. I have a friend who has found what she can do. Although she has multiple chronic diseases, she is president of two different organizations. The smaller group meets in her home so she can attend it. Sometimes she is unable to attend the meetings of the other group. But she uses her computer to send out notices or plan activities.

Don't take on a job that will stress you. Try to think of a small part that you might be able to contribute to the church or organization to which you belong. But, don't feel guilty if you can't do anything at this time.

To simplify our lives and still be active members of a church or organization, we need to find what will work for us at any given time. Sometimes we may be able to do jobs and sometimes we may not. But if we take a job when we are able, we won't feel so guilty when we are unable to take a job.

Chapter 35

Dealing With Insurance Companies

Have you ever been frustrated in attempting to deal with an insurance company? "Some things can't be simplified, and dealing with insurance companies is one of them," Susan said. Several people agreed with Susan. They said that dealing with insurance companies was one part of their lives that they wish could be simplified.

Other people gave these tips on how to simplify your life and be less frustrated when dealing with an insurance company:

- Keep a receipt of all the insurance premiums you have paid. If you have copies of checks, you can place them right in the file with your insurance policy. If you keep records of the checks you have written on the computer, you can have records printed out whenever you want—once a quarter, once every six months, once a year, etc.
- Keep policy and/or claim number handy to give to the person answering the phone or to write on all your correspondence that you send.

- On all correspondence that you send, make sure to write the policy and/or claim number, the date of service, and what service was given.
- Keep copies of all correspondence—what you send and what they send you.
- When talking on the phone to a representative of the insurance company, make sure you write down their name, their phone extension number, what department they work in, the date, the time, and anything that was discussed.
- Be persistent. Mary said, "I think people need to ask questions. If a person is rude or can't give a satisfactory answer, then you need to talk to someone who can." Mona agreed. She said, "If you know there probably will be problems, ask for a supervisor right away. This lets the insurance company personnel know that you are taking charge and you are serious about getting answers."
- If you can't come to an agreement, contact your state insurance commissioner. His/her office might be able to help you.

This morning, I called our automobile insurance company and asked the representative what advice he would give to people calling in. Here is his reply:

- Have policy number ready and be ready to give other pertinent information to verify you are the policyholder.
- Be patient. The representatives want to work with you.
- Remember that the biggest source of conflict is not understanding what your policy actually covers.

The representative added, "Insurance policies really should be written in clearer English."

Based on his suggestions, here are some more recommendations for getting satisfaction from your insurance company:

- Know what your policy covers. If you don't understand the insurance lingo, ask someone to explain it to you. (Sometimes I think insurance terminology is like computer terminology—a foreign language!)
- Make sure your insurance hasn't paid something and then you are asked to pay it. Jill said, "I received a dentist's bill for thirty dollars, when in fact they owed me thirty dollars. I had to have the insurance company call the dentist's billing department and explain that they had already paid!"
- If you have to have a test redone because of the mistake of the physician's office, make sure you or your insurance company don't pay the second bill.
- Check all documents that the insurance company sends to you. Make sure you have received services for all that the insurance company has been billed. Mavis said, "I received a notice that the insurance company was asking for more information on a bill. It was for someone in another state but had my number on it."

It can be frustrating for you to deal with an insurance company. Remember, it can be just as frustrating for the person with whom you are dealing.

I hope that the tips listed above will help to simplify your life when you do have to deal with an insurance company.

Chapter 36

Decorating Your Way

When we have our home decorated or even one corner of it decorated the way we like, it helps us to have a sense of peace and accomplishment within our souls. The trick is for the decorating process not to be so complicated that we don't start or don't finish.

Some of us have a severe disability when it comes to decorating our homes. We have a difficult time trying to pick just the right colors, or we can't tell what something will look like just by visualizing it. We have to have the furniture in place before we can tell if we are going to like it or not—to the disgust of our husbands.

My husband will ask, "Can't you just close your eyelids and see what it will look like?"

"No," I'll answer, "I can't see through my eyelids. It is my eyes that do the seeing, and I have to see what it will look like!"

I think most husbands wouldn't care if the house was decorated the same way forever, because they don't like to move furniture. However, to their wives, their homes are like their clothes, they'd like a change once in a while. A program on television, a picture in a magazine, an advertisement of a sale, or even a visit to a friend's home can "inspire" a decorating attack. My husband groans, "Never mind the inspiring, I'm soon the one perspiring—huffing and puffing as I move the furniture back and forth and back again!"

Louisa has found a way to simplify her decorating. She says, "I simplify my decorating by using what I have and letting my mother-in-law do the work!"

My friend, Lynn, decorates her home beautifully and is on our church decorating committee. Here are some hints she gave me:

- The key to decorating is to use something that you really like, such as a picture, a sofa, or a carpet to determine your color scheme.
- If you can, take a sample of the color with you when you shop.
- Pull colors out of whatever you have chosen for all your accessories. Don't deviate from these colors.
- Use magazines for ideas to help you choose the color and style you like. When something really excites you, copy it.
- Get away from white. White walls are boring. (I asked her if she had been talking to my husband. He wants to paint the walls in our home orange!)

Another friend, Alva, disagrees with Lynn. She says, " I love white walls. I can change my color scheme on the spur of the moment."

Our different personalities, talents, preferences, and finances help determine our preferences and what will work for us.

Mindy said, "Paint doesn't cost much. It can take less time to paint than to wash the walls, and it gives your rooms a new look. Surround yourself with the things you like. Not what some decorator thinks is right. Decorate for yourself and the people you live with. On the other hand, don't have something around because someone gave it to you; if you don't like it, don't use it. Decorate for comfort."

What you find comfortable will change as you go through different periods in your life. When your children have grown and left home, you might want to decorate differently than when they were putting their precious little finger marks around. When your children are small, you may feel the need to get away from home to a bed and breakfast or a motel for a break. However, you may find a sense of peace having your own retreat, even if it is just a rocking chair, somewhere in your house while your family is still at home. Once they have left home, you might fix up your bedroom as your own retreat.

By using what we already had and buying a few more things, my husband and I finally took the money and time and decorated our bedroom into our own retreat. He moaned and groaned the whole time as we moved the furniture around. But now, almost once a week, he mentions how nice it is. Just walking into our bedroom gives us a sense of serenity and calm. It has simplified our life so that now bed and breakfast places no longer hold the charm they once did. We have decided we'd rather travel in a little motor home and see the country than spend the money going to bed and breakfasts.

Decide for yourself what you need to feel comfortable and special in your own home. Here are some tips from other people on how to help you achieve your decorating goals:

- Be absolutely sure you want and need something before you buy it. Especially if it is a large item like a couch that you will have to live with for a long time.
- Use what you have.
- Decorate for your lifestyle. If you will be moving often, don't buy heavy furniture.
- Keep copies of pictures and samples of materials in a large binder where you can get at them easily.

Hopefully one of these ideas will help you simplify your decorating. Have fun decorating! It can be fun to move the furniture around—even if it ends back where you had it in the first place!

Chapter 37

Tickle Your Funny Bone

Do you need to tickle your funny bone? Your life will be simplified if you learn to laugh at yourself. Especially if you are having a bad day or going through an emotionally draining experience, a good laugh can help you survive.

My friend Marian is a great example. Marian copes with multiple autoimmune diseases and most of the time can do little more than sit in her chair. Those of us who are blessed by her friendship have had our day brightened by her humor. The following is a note she sent me by e-mail. I'm copying it exactly as she wrote it:

"I haven't been having a good day today. I'm beginning to think, I need a body guard. I'm not safe anywhere. Following is the tale: < hear Bonanza music and galloping horses' hooves here>

"I started out the day with a fun migraine. Then, about 12:15 this afternoon, when I finished teaching my second on-line class for today (and I only knew ahead of time that I was teaching the second one), I put a hot pack in the micro-wave to heat and then hopped in my electric wheelchair to go get the mail out at the road. I got down the front walk about fifteen feet and a bug flew in my right eye.

"Now I've had bugs fly in my eye before, but this hurt worse than usual, and then there was this horrible stench too. I whirled around and got back into the house and drove to the bathroom where I needed to leap out of the wheelchair to get to the sink and water to wash my eye out.

"Sounds easy enough. But I caught the edge of my slipper under one wheel of the wheelchair and didn't know it, so I pitched forward and landed on my knees and wrists. <sigh>

"I scrambled into the bathroom and sat on the chair I keep in there and swished water through my eye in my cupped hand. While I was doing that, I grabbed the bathroom phone and called the "O" operator and asked her to call Poison Control, which she did. (I think she was scared, because her voice shook and she said, "I'm hurrying as fast as I can, and I'll stay on the line until they answer.")

"When Poison Control answered the pre-recorded voice said if this is an emergency press one. The only problem is that the phone in the bathroom is the only tele in the house that isn't digital so pressing one didn't do anything. So I was stuck with the option of hanging on until some operator got around to answering. <slosh, slosh, continues>

"Finally I got someone and she didn't like the way I was washing my eye. I tried her method, but between my weak muscles and not being able to stand up, etc. I couldn't make it work.

"Anyway, I ended up washing my eye for fifteen minutes and then collapsed on the hospital bed. Kerry [her husband] got home after about fifteen minutes, called Poison Control back as instructed, and she had him take me to the emergency medical care place.

"I had a large corneal abrasion around the bottom of my cornea in my right eye from 4 o'clock to 8 o'clock. Just what I needed!

"The doctor thought it was a good idea to put antibiotic drops in my eye. I asked about it because my immune system is so suppressed and I know that after all that washing I'd be in danger of getting an infection—and I don't know the whereabouts of that wretched bug. He put a patch over my eye. I also got him to give me the little bottle with the rest of the antibiotic drops. No sense wasting it since he says I need to come back tomorrow and after the patch comes off I'll need antibiotic eye drops. Besides, if I don't use it for my eye, surely it could be used for rubber stamping.<GGG>

"It's now 7:30 p.m. and here I sit with my eye patched, my eye is weeping and hurting like fury. And my knees hurt too.

"By the way, I still have my migraine.

"Just about the time one thinks things can't get worse, THEY DO! Maybe I should get Kerry to pack me away in cotton balls. He'd probably snag me with a fingernail or something in the process. <GGG>

"I guess there's one good thing—it was a bug and not a bird. <g>

"Calamity Jane"

What has Marian done here? She has told me what happened because she knew I would be interested. However, she added the humor. If we could all tickle our funny bones—laugh at ourselves like she did, we might be able to relax and our lives would be simpler.

Chapter 38

Skip Over the Bumps

Six-year-old Amy was jumping back and forth across the speed bumps on the road in front of her mobile home. "Amy, what are you doing? asked her mother.

"I'm just skipping over the bumps," Amy replied.

Like Amy, we need to "skip over the bumps" that we meet when we are trying to simplify our lives. Instead of becoming discouraged when we can't complete a simplifying project, maybe we need to try:

- Doing it a different way
- Leaving it for a while
- Stopping it altogether
- Going on to another project
- Taking a break from simplifying

So let's skip over the bumps and make our lives easier. Let's find more peace and comfort and joy in living by simplifying our lives.